AGRI MECHANICA

Career Support Guide for
Agricultural Engineers

Er. RATHINAVEL S

notionpress.com

INDIA • SINGAPORE • MALAYSIA

CONTENTS

FOREWORD

Agricultural Engineering interventions have contributed in enhancing productivity, reduction in cost of production, timeliness in farm operations and reduction in drudgery of farm workers, The future of Agricultural Engineering, particularly in the fields of Farm  Machinery and Renewable Energy, holds immense potential and promise. These disciplines are at the forefront of addressing some of the most pressing challenges facing our world today i.e ensuring food security, promoting sustainable practices, and advancing technological innovations. It is in this context that the title *'Agri Mechanica'* is critical and vital

Designed to serve as a comprehensive guide for Agricultural Engineering students and educators, this book covers an extensive range of topics across 18 well-structured chapters. Its primary aim is not just to impart knowledge but to equip readers with the tools and skills necessary to excel in competitive exams, interviews, and their future careers. The approach is holistic, combining traditional learning with contemporary examination trends.

The inclusion of essential terminology and keywords serves a dual purpose i.e it introduces new concepts and reinforces existing knowledge. Moreover, the book's relevance extends beyond academic preparation. It addresses the expectations of Agricultural machinery industry recruiters, providing interview prompts and situational questions that mirrors the real demands of professional world. The content in the book aligns with industry standards, ensuring that readers are not only exam-ready but also career-ready.

I commend the author for this invaluable contribution in the field of farm machinery and renewable energy. The effort and dedication put into compiling this comprehensive resource are praise worthy. I am confident that the information presented on different aspects in this compilation will be beneficial to students, teachers and other stakeholders in analyzing needs and requirements of these vital areas of Agricultural Engineering Best wishes to all readers for their academic and professional success.

30.07.2024

Dr.R.KAVITHA,Ph.D,

Professor and Head,

Department of Farm Machinery & Power Engg.,

Agricultural Engineering College and Research Institute,

Tamil Nadu Agricultural University, Coimbatore – 641 003

Tamil Nadu, India.

PREFACE

This book is designed for Agricultural Engineering students and educators specializing in Farm Machinery and Renewable Energy disciplines. It comprises 18 chapters covering a broad spectrum of farm machinery and key renewable energy topics.

While not tailored specifically for competitive exams, this book aims to assist individuals in preparing for such assessments, interviews, and career challenges. It presents a variety of question types including situational, statement selection, matching, management questions, interview prompts, alongside traditional true/false and multiple-choice formats. These questions are intended to familiarize readers with contemporary examination trends and enhance their readiness for diverse contests. The questions range from basic to advanced technical levels, catering to a diverse audience.

Although the book primarily consists of questions and answers, the included terminology serves as essential keywords that may introduce new concepts to the reader. Its purpose is to stimulate the acquisition of knowledge rather than provide direct learning.

The content addresses the rigorous nature of various competitive exams such as ICAR PG/Ph.D. entrance examinations, ICAR-ASRB National Eligibility Tests, ARS exams, state-level competitive exams, and university entrance examinations. Interview prompts are structured based on perception of farm machinery industry recruiters.

Postgraduate study in any discipline signifies a higher level of expertise and comprehension within one's specialization. This book aims to facilitate advanced knowledge acquisition and understanding to get specialized in agricultural mechanization sector.

I trust this book will be of significant value to its readers and contribute to their success in their academic and professional pursuits. Any feedback for improving the quality and betterment of the book as well as farm machinery discipline is invited pivoting this book. I extend our sincere gratitude for any constructive feedback and apologize for any inadvertent errors. Thank you for your interest and support.

Best wishes for your academic and career endeavours.

Er.Rathinavel S

30.07.2024

ACKNOWLEDGEMENT

Agricultural Engineering College & Research Institute, TNAU, Kumulur

Department of Bioenergy, AEC&RI, TNAU, Coimbatore

Department of Farm Machinery & Power Engg., Kelappaji College of Agricultural Engg. & Technology, KAU, Thavanur

Department of Farm Machinery & Power Engg., AEC&RI, TNAU, Coimbatore

Indian Council of Agricultural Research, New Delhi

Mentoring Professors & Scientists

*Dr.B.Suthakar, Dr.R.Mythili, Dr.P.Dhananchezhiyan,
Dr.M.Saravana Kumar, Dr.S.A.Ramjani, Dr.A.P.Mohankumar,
Dr.J.John Gunasekaran, Dr.R.Mahendran, Dr.P.Subramanian,
Dr.S.Sriramajayam, Dr.R.Angeeswaran, Dr.S.Pugazhendhi,*

*Dr.Jayan P R, Er.Shivaji K P, Er.Sindhu Bhaskar,
Dr.Manoj Mathew, Dr.Manohar Jesudas, Dr.R.Kavitha,
Dr.A.Surendrakumar, Dr.A.Kamaraj*

Supporting Professors & Scientists

Dr.P.Vijayakumari, Dr.P.Kamaraj, Dr.P.K.Padmanathan, Dr.S.Thambidurai, Dr.B.Shridar, Er.Sanchu Sukumaran, Dr.Joby Bastian, Dr.T.Senthilkumar, Dr.R.Thiyagarajan,

Dr.D.Ramesh, Dr.Carolin Rathinakumari,

Class mates, Batch mates, Seniors and Juniors, Teaching and non-teaching faculties of

TNAU - Kumulur & Coimbatore & KAU - Thavanur

My friends, family and Lord

திருக்குறள்
(Thirukkural)

பால்: பொருட்பால் **(Porutpaal)**

அதிகாரம்: உழவு

Chapter: Farming

சுழன்றும்ஏர்ப் பின்னது உலகம் அதனால்
உழந்தும் உழவே தலை.

(suzhandrum-Erp pinnadhu ulagam adhanaal
uzhandhum uzhavae thalai)

**Howe'er they roam, the world must follow still the plougher's team;
Though toilsome, culture of the ground as noblest toil esteem.**

உழுவார் உலகத்தார்க்கு ஆணிஅஃ தாற்றாது
எழுவாரை எல்லாம் பொறுத்து.

(uzhuvaar ulagaththaarkku aaNi-aq thaatraadhu
ezhuvaarai ellaam poRuththu)

**The ploughers are the linch-pin of the world; they bear
Them up who other works perform, too weak its toils to share.**

உழுதுண்டு வாழ்வாரே வாழ்வார்மற் றெல்லாம்
தொழுதுண்டு பின்செல் பவர்.

(uzhudhuNdu vaazhvaarae vaazhvaarmaR Rellaam
thozhudhuNdu pinsel pavar)

Who ploughing eat their food, they truly live:
The rest to others bend subservient, eating what they give.

பலகுடை நீழலும் தங்குடைக்கீழ்க் காண்பர்
அலகுடை நீழ லவர்

(palakudai neezhalum thangutaikkeezhk kaaNpar
alakutai neezha lavar)

O'er many a land they 'll see their monarch reign,
Whose fields are shaded by the waving grain.

இரவார் இரப்பார்க்கொன்று ஈவர் கரவாது
கைசெய்தூண் மாலை யவர்

(iravaar irappaarkkondru eevar karavaadhu
kaiseydhooN maalai yavar)

They nothing ask from others, but to askers give,
Who raise with their own hands the food on which they live.

உழவினார் கைம்மடங்கின் இல்லை விழைவதூஉம்
விட்டேம்என் பார்க்கும் நிலை.

(uzhavinaar kaimmatangin illai vizhaivadhooum
vittaemen paarkkum nilai)

For those who 've left what all men love no place is found,
When they with folded hands remain who till the ground.

தொடிப்புழுதி கஃசா உணக்கின் பிடித்தெருவும்
வேண்டாது சாலப் படும்

(thotippuzhudhi kaqsaa uNakkin pitiththeruvum
vaeNtaadhu saalap padum)

Reduce your soil to that dry state, When ounce is quarter-ounce's
weight;

Without one handful of manure, Abundant crops you thus secure.

ஏரினும் நன்றால் எருவிடுதல் கட்டபின்
நீரினும் நன்றதன் காப்பு

(Erinum nandraal eruvidudhal kattapin
neerinum nandradhan kaappu)

**To cast manure is better than to plough;
Weed well; to guard is more than watering now.**

செல்லான் கிழவன் இருப்பின் நிலம்புலந்து
இல்லாளின் ஊடி விடும்

(sellaan kizhavan iruppin nilampulandhu
illaaLin ooti vidum)

**When master from the field aloof hath stood;
Then land will sulk, like wife in angry mood.**

இலமென்று அசைஇ இருப்பாரைக் காணின்
நிலமென்னும் நல்லாள் நகும்.

(ilamendru asaii iruppaaraik kaaNin
nilamennum nallaaL nakum)

**The earth, that kindly dame, will laugh to see,
Men seated idle pleading poverty.**

CHAPTER 1
ENGINES & POWER

1. Above what engine speed, HSD may be used? (250/ 500/ 750/ 2000)

   750 RPM

2. Efficiency of petrol engine (0.25 to 32%/ 25 to 320%/ 25 to 32.0%/ 25.0 to 3.2%)

   25 to 32.0%

3. Why five cylinder engines were not common?

4. Give one of the commercially available stroke lengths of tractor engine

5. In 2009, a policy made mandatory blending at least 5% of ethanol with petrol. Name the Policy

   National Policy on Biofuels

6. Name the Automatic motor vehicle transmission which is able to transmit power to two different places at the same time and even control amount of power sent to each output source.

   Split torque transmission

7. Which is the most popular clutch in four wheelers?   (Fictional clutch/ Perma clutch/ Single clutch/ Frictional clutch)

   Friction clutch

8. What is the other name of TDC (Top dead Centre)?

   HDC – Head Dead Centre

9. Other name of BDC is CDC. What is the full form of CDC?
   CDC – Crank Dead Centre

10. What is the speed of the engine at high idle point?
    Higher

11. What is mean by torque reserve?
    Difference between the peak torque of an engine and the torque at rated speed

12. Why BS V skipped in India for Indian Motor Vehicles?
    India is following Euro Standards, by the time of deciding next stage, Euro Standards was in BS VI, but India was in BS IV. Hence the norms were directly upgraded to BS VI.

13. Which is the fuel used for tractors in earlier times?
    First tractor built - Gasoline/Petrol
    Kerosene, Distillate, LPG
    All others replaced by Diesel (by 1960's)

14. What is distillate? The term association with fuel.
    Distillate is a petroleum fraction comprising of diesel fuel and oils, derived from distillation of crude petroleum.

15. A fuel which is highly resistant to detonation is?

16. What is meant by square engine?
    The Engine having stroke bore ratio as 1 is called as square engine

17. In what type of transmission, there is no need for differential?
    Hydrostatic transmission

18. Expand CVT?
    Continuously Variable Transmission

19. What is the Friction Material used in clutches? (Ferrari/ Ferrado/ Ferhenheit/ Fullerin)

    Ferrado

20. Lay shaft is otherwise called as? (Main shaft/ Bore shaft/ Counter shaft/ All the above)

    Counter shaft

21. What is the Calorific value of diesel?

    HSD - 10550 Kcal/l

    LSD - 10300 Kcal/l

22. If the clearance of a valve is too large, the operation of the valve will become?

    Noisy

23. When 4WD can be disengaged?

    A. On roads

    B. Without any draft load,

    C. Free moving situations

    (Any of the situations of A, B or C/ Situation with all three cases together/ A only/ A and C only)

    Any of the situations of A, B or C

24. Which type of engine does a tractor have? (Square/ Under square/ Over square/ Circular)

    Overhead

25. Wet clutches are used in tractors. (True/False)

    True

26. What is the commercial gear transmission systems used for tractors?

    Sliding mesh,

    Sliding mesh constant mesh hybrid,

    Synchronous mesh also interested recently

27. Where does the parking brake acts? (Front axle/ Steering/ Flywheel/ Rear axle)

    Rear axle

28. Bendix Drive is a component of? (Gear box/ Electrical system/ Starting motor/ Steering)

    Starting motor

29. What is the octane number of Hydrogen? (Greater than 12/ Greater than 120/ Less than 120/ Less than 10)

    Greater than 120

30. What may be the brake fluid mixture used in the hydraulic brake system which is based on Pascal's law?

    Glycerin and Alcohol

31. Replacement for most of the ICE's in next decades will be?

32. Boost is an energy drink only and not an increase in pressure provided by the compressor in turbocharger. Is the statement is wrong?

    Yes

33. Turbocharger is effective, when?

    Governor's maximum load

34. What are the levels of mechanization?

    Low (Manual)

    Medium or fair (Animal)

    High (Mechanical)

35. (A) Globally 70% of the land holdings are small (<1 ha).

    (B) The average farm size in India is small (1.16 ha).

(Both the statements are correct and related/ Both the statements are wrong but related/ Both the statements are not related but correct/ Both are wrong and no relation)

Both the statements are correct and related

36. Product of gauge pressure (kPa) and flow rate (Ls^{-1}) gives fluid power in (W/kW/hp/MW)

    W

37. i.   Power, P = (FS/3.6) where F is force and S is Speed

    ii.   Force in Newton

    iii. Speed in meter per second

    (No match between the statements/All three matching together/i is incorrect but ii and iii are correct/ ii is not matching with i and iii)

    All three matching together

38. (A) North-eastern states have negligible mechanization. (B) Hill agriculture, which covers about 20 % of cultivated land, has little access to mechanization.

    (Both the statements are correct and related/ Both the statements are wrong but related/ Both the statements are not related but correct/ Both are wrong and no relation)

    Both the statements are correct and related

39. Which is the combination of F and I head in engines?

    F head engine

40. F head engines are mostly used engine type. (True/False)

    False

41. A. Diesel engine converts 30% of useful work into heat

    B. Diesel engine converts 30% of heat into useful work

C. Diesel engine converts 80% of heat into useful work

D. Diesel engine converts 80% of useful work into heat

Incorrect statement(s) are (a,b,d/a,c,d/b only/c only)

a,c,d

42. Closed circuit radiator system operates under a pressure of about?

(5 kg cm^{-2}/0.5 kg cm^{-2}/0.05 kg cm^{-2}/None of the above)

0.5 kg cm^{-2}

43. Neither a pump nor a thermostat is used in thermosiphon system. The statement is (Associated with Forced circulation cooling system/Incorrect/Associated with Forced circulation lubrication system/None of the above)

None of the above

44. Camshaft for 4 cylinder engine has how many numbers of cams? (4/2/8/16), How many for each valve? (2,3,1,4)

8, 1

45. If heaviest shaft in the engine is written in reverse spelt, it is? (tfahsleehw/tfahsnori/tfahsmac/ tfahsknarc)

tfahsknarc

(Crankshaft)

46. Pick the odd one out (Eicher Good Earth/Motor cycle/Scooter/ Maruti 800 Car)

Maruti 800 Car

(Maruti 800 car is multiple cylinder engine, while others are single cylinder engines)

47. Now-a-days vertical engines are used in general (True/False)

True

48. **Match the following**

S. No.	A	M. No.	B
1	High exhaust temperature	A	Constant volume
2	High maintenance cost		
3	Low exhaust temperature	B	Constant pressure
4	Low maintenance cost		

Ans: 1-b, 2-b, 3-a, 4-a

49. **Match the following with connection**

S. No.	A	M. No.	B	C. No.	C
1	Weight per hp	A	Big/More/Higher	i	2 S
2	Vibration				
3	Mechanical efficiency	B	Small/Less/Lower	ii	4 S
4	Thermal efficiency				
5	Size				

Options: a) 1-b-i, 2-b-i, 3-a-i, 4-b-i, 5-b-i

b) 1-a-ii, 2-a-ii, 3-b-ii, 4-a-ii, 5-a-ii

c) 1-b-I, 2-a-ii, 3-b-ii, 4-b-i, 5-a-ii

d) all are correct

Ans: all are correct

50. The term hybrid is associated with a tractor component? (a.Engine b.Gearbox c.Rice d. Tyre e.Seat) Options: (a,b,c and e/a and b/a alone/a and c)

a and b

CHAPTER 2

TRACTORS

1. Why tractor front wheels are smaller than rear?
    Better steering

2. In India, AC Cabins were launched for tractors. (Soon/ True/ Not at all/ Existing from 90's)
    True

3. Which is the least efficient power output in tractor?
    Drawbar

4. What is meant by ALT? (Computer key/Antilift tractor/Anti Linear Term/Alternative linear Transmission)
    Antilift tractor

5. What is MFWD?
    Mechanical Front Wheel Drive

6. AutoTrac is the feature of (Rotary tiller/PTO/ Tractor/All of the above)
    Tractor

7. In India, what is the commonly used cylinder count in tractors?
    3, 4 cylinders

8. Three point linkage system was invented by? (Ramasamy/ Thirukurungudi Vengaram Sundaram/Harry Ferguson/John Froelich)
    Harry Ferguson

9. Where does tractor pulley located?
    Tractor's Right, Left or Rear side

10. Give the common PTO speed and spline count combinations
    4 (6 splines – 540 RPM, 6 splines – 750 RPM, 20 splines – 1000 RPM, 21 splines – 1000 RPM)

11. How to measure PTO power output?
    Dynamometer

12. What is the value of hardness for PTO shaft?
    Splined portions shall have a hardness of 48 HRC

13. What are the available diameters for PTO? (35 mm/ 39 mm/ 45 mm/ Both A and C)
    Both A and C

14. What is the toe-in range for tractors? (1 to 10 mm/ 7 to 10 nm/ 7 to 10 mm/ 1 to 10 nm)
    7 to 10 mm

15. Name the applications for multi reverse PTO

16. The location of PTO from the drawbar should be at a distance of? (2 meter/ 20 meter/ 0.2 meter/ 0.02 meter)
    0.2 meter

17. Give two advanced technologies in tractor regards to tractor stability?
    Antilift technology, 4WD

18. What is the advantage of swinging drawbar?
    Short turns are possible with the attached machines wider than tractor

19. Low inflation pressure of a tractor tyre may results in
    Shearing of nozzle

20. Overinflation of a tractor tyre may result in? (Slow wear of tyres/ Rapid wear of tyres/ No wear of tyres/ Either A or C)
    Rapid wear of tyres

21. What type of treads can grip extremely soft soils? (Modern/ Deeper/ Shallow/ Hollow)
    Deeper treads

22. At what intervals, the tractor wheel axle bearings should be washed and repacked? (1.2 months/ 120 months/ 12 months/ 24 months)
    12 months

23. The starter of a tractor is said not to be applied continuously for longer than 15 seconds. Why?
    It causes Sulphation, warping of plates, and crumbling out of active material.

24. (A) States ranking higher in tractor density is in North India. (B) TAFE tractors headquarters is in south India.
    (A is correct and B is not a valid reason on A/ A is wrong/ B is wrong and not A is correct/ A is valid reason when B holds right)

    A is correct and B is not a valid reason on A

    (Haryana and Punjab ranks top in tractor density in India. TAFE head office located at Chennai)

25. India is the largest tractor exporter. The statement is (False/ Expired statement/ True/ Inverse)

26. 'Uber for tractors' and 'Hello tractor' are the applications for hiring tractors. (True/False)

    True

27. Track type tractors don't have more than 10% slip. (Statement is logically correct/ Statement don't have meaning/ Statement is not grammatically correct/ None of the above). Give explanation

    Statement is logically correct.

    Since the value 5% (actual limit value for track type tractors slip) is within 10% (value mentioned in the statement), said to be logically correct

28. A. Gear shift lever should be in neutral position before cranking the engine

    B. Should not refuel a tractor in running condition

    C. Never drive a tractor if you are less than 21 years old

    D. Never drive the tractor without music system

    E. Tractor should not be started near straw

    Identify the correct statements (A,B,C,E/ A,B,C,D,E/ A,B,E/C,D)

    A,B,E

29. Factors contributing to the tractor field efficiency were

    Unloading time

    Loading time and Refueling

    Repair

    Maintenance

    Machine adjustments

    (a,c,d and e/a,b,c,d and e/d and e only/a,b,d and e)

    a,b,d and e

30. Tractor tyre pressure should be checked during (Purchase/when the vehicle is working/rainy season/All the above)

    When the vehicle is working

31. Swinging drawbar has the main advantage taking longer turns (True/False)

    False

32. If one of the tractor tyre is locked, then the other tyre speed will be doubled (True/False)

    True

33. Path of power from engine to wheels is called as (Electric train/ Metro train/Gear system/Power train)

    Power train

34. Incompatibility between the tractor and grain harvesters' track gauges, resulted in an early focus on the advantages of the wide-span field tractor called?

    Gantry tractor

35. **Match the following**

S. No.	A	M. No.	B
1	FARMS	a	TAFE
2	Agro Solutions	b	GoI
3	JFarm	c	Sonalika

    Ans: 1-b, 2-c, 3-a

36. **Match the following**

S. No.	A	M. No.	B
1	TRRINGO	a	Tamilnadu
2	Uzhavan	b	Karnataka
3	Krushi Yantradhare	c	M&M

    Ans: 1-c, 2-a, 3-b

37. Match the following

S. No.	A	M. No.	B
1	Mast	a	Front wheel
2	Steering knuckle	b	Protection
3	Fender	c	Upper hitch point

Ans: 1-c, 2-a, 3-b

38. Match the following

S. No.	A	M. No.	B
1	Battery cell	a	Electric pressure
2	Clutches of farm tractors	b	Gear type pump
3	Lubrication system	c	Friction

Ans: 1-a, 2-b, 3-c

39. Match the following

S. No.	A	M. No.	B
1	Pinion and bull gear	a	Apportioning
2	Hydraulic pump	b	70 to 140 kg cm^{-2}
3	Differential	c	Reduction

Ans: 1-c, 2-b, 3-a

40. Match the following

S. No.	A	M. No.	B
1	Centre of pull	a	All drafting load is centralized
2	Line of draft	b	Ahead of axle
3	Centre of load	c	Center of pull to the centre of implement load

Ans: 1-b, 2-c, 3-a

41. Perma clutch associated with damage to drivelines (True/False)

    True

42. a. Perma clutch – Protection, b. EVT – Electric Variable Transmission, c. IVT – Infinitely Variable Transmission (a,b,c are false and related to tractor segment/a and b only true and related to tractor segment/all are true and does not related to tractor segment/all are true and related to tractor segment)

    All are true and related to tractor segment

43. **Match the following**

S. No.	A	M. No.	B
1	Power shuttle	a	Flexible hoses
2	Hydraulic steering	b	Constant mesh
3	Collor shift	c	Power Reverser

    Ans: 1-c, 2-a, 3-b

44. What does OOS stands for?

    Open Operator Station

45. What does IT4 and FT4 associated with? (Emissions/Gearbox/ Hydraulics/ROPS)

    Emissions

46. What does TREM means?

    Tractor Emission Norms

47. BS TREM standards and timeline for implementations are set by the ministry of? (Central Climate Control Board/Environment, Forestry and Climate change/Agriculture and farmers welfare/ Electronics and Languages)

    Environment, Forestry and Climate change

48. Which country made the first tractor?

    Iowa

49. What does FOPS stands for? (Falling Object Protective Structure/ First Object Production System/ Flight Objective and Position Surfacing/ F. O. Panneer Samy)

    Falling Object Protective Structure

50. What does the colors of tractors signifies? (Competition/ Visibility/Safety/All the above)

    All the above

51. [Bearing - Play inspection] [Undercarriage – cleaning] [Air filter – replacement] [Clutch – Adjustment] [Hydraulic fluid - Level check] – How many pairs are correct? (4/3/5/6)

    5

52. **Match the following**

S. No.	A	M. No.	B
1	New Holland	a	Mason Vaugh
2	Pulleys	b	Pressure adjustment
3	Tire	c	Lubrication
4	Agricultural Engineering	d	Farm Tractor
5	Belt	e	Tension adjustment
6	Engine		Tune up
7	PTO Shaft		Alignment check

Ans: 1-d, 2-c, 3-b, 4-a, 5-e

53. What drone feature is vital for assessing crop water stress, assisting tractors in precise irrigation scheduling?

    A. Correct: Thermal Imaging

    B. Wrong: Acoustic Imaging, Electromagnetic Sensing, Inertial Navigation

The above question has answer on A (Yes/No)

Yes

54. Which specific aspect of drone software integration is essential for ensuring precise tractor navigation during planting?
Geofencing

55. Which specific tractor modification is necessary to utilize real-time data from drones? (Telemetry/Hydraulic processor/micro processor/Antenna)
Telemetry

56. Which feature of autonomous tractors is enhanced by using drone-generated 3D terrain models for accurate planting depth? Answer is a phrase XX YY words. Options for XX and YY are given in the following table. Whether the XX answer and YY answer belongs to same option number? (Yes/ No/ Partially/ All the above)

Option	XX	YY
1	Pitch	Connect
2	Depth	Communicate
3	Speed	Convince
4	Auto	Control

No

57. Differences between

    a. Position control and draft control

    b. Mechanical front wheel drive and independent front wheel drive

    c. Open centre and closed centre hydraulic system

58. What do you know about 'trahere'?

59. The purpose of not having deep treads in tractor tyres is to have more contact area (Yes/No/Tractor tyres have deep treads/ Tractors tyres don't have deep treads)

    Tractor tyres have deep treads

60. What is the purpose of creeper gear?

61. Give some other names for a tractor.

62. Specify a power range of a tractor for your own farm field or your most relevant farm field.

63. Give an outline for tractor based farming system with minimal or no soil compaction for any cereal crop.

64. If you are running a custom hiring centre with number of tractors, how you will monitor the operations of tractors at various locations from your mobile or laptop?

65. What are the ways to reduce fuel consumption in heavy machinery applications?

66. A large farmer is purchasing a tractor for the first time. He has field operations, hauling, power generation applications. What model/make tractor you will suggest for this large farmer?

67. A medium farmer needs a economically least costing tractor and use. What tractor I have to suggest to the farmer?

68. Consider a situation where you are working in a tractor company as sales manager. A model of tractor is at high demand, so presently only one tractor is available with you for sale. An unknown farmer with good economic status approached first for the tractor. Next, a known farmer (relative or friend of you), who is poor in economic status approaching for the same. Now, to whom you will allocate the tractor?

69. A farmer is not convinced of purchasing a mini tractor, where it was the most suitable model/make. He is demanding for heavier tractor. Whether you will allocate a mini tractor or heavier one?

70. What is the importance of colour in tractor appearance?

71. Name a 10 different tractor brands in India.

72. Did you or your family own a tractor at your house? What is the criteria followed for selection of the brand you own?

73. How to increase the adoption of electric tractors in your state? Give a smart tactics.

74. If you are the state level manager for a new tractor brand in the state you appointed. How you will set the sales outlets in the state?

75. What is the most important drawback in Indian tractors to be researched with high priority?

76. What is the very latest and breakthrough technology in Indian tractor industry?

77. What are the unnecessary/least used - system/technology in modern tractors?

78. Give tips to maintain a very high resale value of a tractor.

79. How many tractors may be available (roughly) in India as of now?

80. What is the most important feature of any foreign tractor to be imparted or followed in India.

81. What is the importance of clay model in industrial design?

82. Tractor tyre pressure might influence

    A. Rolling resistance

    B. Fuel consumption

C. Seat alignment

D. Running cost

(Both A and C/ Both B and D/ All 4/ A, B and D only)

A, B and D only

83. What are the prime reasons for tractor accidents?

84. State the height range of Indian tractors.

85. Describe about tractor front wheel differential.

86. Precision tracking of a tractor can be done using (GPS/IMU/ Geoencoders/All the above)
All the above

87. Give a conceptual framework for automatic hitch system in tractors.

88. Give the classification of Indian tractor based on power, application and drive.

89. How many numbers of lights present in a common tractor?

90. Indian tractors may weigh in the range of (0.1 ton/ 1 ton/ 50 ton/ 10 ton)
1 ton

CHAPTER 3

FARM IMPLEMENTS & MACHINERY (PART I)

1. What is meant by a Paraplow?
   Type of Subsoiler with slanted legs on 45 degree

2. In seed drill cum fertilizer applicators generally may have the no. of rows of construction in the range of? (1 to 20 no. of rows/ 20 to 30 no. of rows/ 1 to 13 no. of rows/ 5 to 11 no. of rows)
   1 to 13 no. of rows

3. Left hand type mould board plough is rare in the India. Why?
   The bullocks are trained usually to take left while ploughing

4. Spike tooth harrow can stir the soil upto the meters of? (5/0.5/0.05/1)
   0.05

5. What may be the weight of the subsoiler? (4000 to 5000 grams/4000 kg to 5000 kg/400000 to 500000 grams/40 to 500000 grams)
   400000 to 500000 grams

6. The implement consisting of vertically rotating blades are called as?
   Auger plough

7. Tractor drawn cotton uprooter is powered by? (Drawbar/Tractor PTO/Battery/None)

    Tractor PTO

8. One way plough is also known as vertical disc plough. (True/False)

    True

9. Mention a few advancements in Subsoiler

    Winged Subsoiler,

    Subsoiler with modified tynes,

    Subsoiler with lesser weight

10. Bose Plough used in rainfed agriculture of many states is developed from? (Megalaya/Kerala/Adilabad/Karnataka)

    Karnataka

11. Subsurface ploughs are heavier than chisel plough. (True/False)

    True

12. Can thermal spraying hardening process in shovels have less wear comparing electroplating hardening process? (Yes/No)

    Yes

13. Range of vertical suction in MB plough?

    Tractor drawn MB Plough: 3-5 mm

    Animal drawn MB Plough: 12- 20 mm

14. Which implement has negative draft? (Rotovator/ Wood chipper/ Duck foot shovel/ Planker)

    Rotovator

15. What may be the useful life of wooden planker? (2/5.5/10/100 years)

    10 years

16. Name a place in Tamilnadu/Kerala manufacturing Indigenous ploughs.

    Melur, Madurai Region

17. The primary objective in establishing field pattern is maximizing the amount of field travel.

    Engineer D conveyed the above statement to Engineer K. Engineer K now has to agree/deny the statement?

    Deny the statement.

18. Mention some of the field patterns

    Round, Turn strips, headland pattern, inland, circuitous pattern, alternation pattern

19. Name a plough involving most complex field pattern.

    MB Plough

20. i. Towed hitch – Single point hitch - Has own transport wheels

    ii. Two point hitch – Semi mounted hitch - Restricts relative movement in horizontal plane

    iii. Mounted hitch – Three point hitch - Has own transport wheels

    Scholar A said there is a error in (ii) has an error. Scholar B refused to scholar A and stated that (iii) has error. Now the Scholar C has to decide whose statement is correct. What should be the decision of Scholar C?

    (Scholar A is correct but Scholar B can also be accepted/ Scholar B is only correct/Scholar A is only correct/ Both are wrong and required better understanding)

    Scholar B is only correct

21.   A. Revolving scraper   -   Contour ploughing

B. Radial needle type bearing -   Standard disc plough

C. Reversible disc plough   -   Thrust bearing

Pairs are (Correct/Incorrect)

Incorrect

22.   A. Vertical clevis   -   Line of draft

B. Horizontal clevis   -   Line of pull

Pairs are (Correct/Incorrect)

Incorrect

23.   I   II

A. Cultivator   -   Leaves the field level

B. Reversible Disc Plough   -   Killling weeds

C. Tilt angle   -   Degree of pulverization

D. Rotovator   -   Treader

(Column I have relevant matches in column II and paired/ Column I have relevant matches in column II but not paired/ Column I don't have relevant matches in column II and not paired/ Column I don't have relevant matches in column II but paired)

Column I have relevant matches in column II but not paired

24.   Choose the incorrect answer. Harrow suitable for stony fields is (Spring tooth/ Harrow with steel leaf/ Spike tooth/ Both A and B)

Spike tooth

25.   Long fields are recommended to be ploughed by (Gathering one season and Casting two season/ Gathering two season and Casting two season/ Gathering three season and

Casting one season/ Gathering one season and Casting one season)

Gathering one season and Casting one season

26. What is you know about Controlled Traffic Farming (CTF)?

27. When the reel of a harvesting machine touches the crop stalk on working, it should not comprise of? (Horizontal component/ Vertical component/ Blade/ None)
Horizontal Component

28. Normally the reel axis must be how much distance ahead of the cutting bar? (15 to 30 cm/ 150 to 300 mm/ 200 to 400 mm/ Both A and B)
Both A and B

29. Good combine operators can keep losses down to 97%. If this is not true, what was the correct numerical value to be replaced?
3

30. What is the steering mechanism in power tillers?
Clutches on both wheels

31. Why eyebolt (above the engine) is provided on a power tiller? (Clear vision/ Shakti Uzhavan design/ Google sinking/ Transport support)
Transport support

32. What may be the average cost of power tiller in India?

33. Height range of airplane spraying may be at? (90 cm to 1500 cm/ 900 cm to 150 m/ 9 m to 15000 cm/ 900 cm to m)
900 cm to 15 m

34. Combine harvesters are preferred to work during _______ for wheat crop. (Mid day/ Night/ 15 days after complete maturity/ May month)Explain.

    Due to lower temperature, night time may have less losses

35. Japanese type Walk behind harvesting machine, can work on crops lodged even at 20^0, with a knitting mechanism. The machine is called as? (Reaper/ Cotton to thread maker/ Reaper binder/ Both A and B)

    Reaper binder

36. Name the some different types of horticultural machines

    Rotating disc mower, Lawn Mower,

    Auger digger, Post hole digger

    Media/Pot filling Machine

    Seeder, Planter, Transplanters

    Lopping machine

    Pluckers, Graders, Harvesters, Diggers

    Elevators and Loaders

    Shredders, Clump removers

37. Is the lawn tractor and turf terrace are same machine?

    No

38. What is the turning radius of Turf terrace? (1.2 m/ 2.1 m/ 0.01 m/ 0)

    0

39. Is lawn aeration is necessary? How it can be mechanized?

    Yes, Roller lawn aerator (Manual or Tractor)

40. Based on blade type, lawn mowers can be classified as? (Reel and like/ Reel and rotary/ Rotary and Lion/ Circular and V shaped)
Reel type and Rotary blade type

41. Pineapple harvesting can be done by? (Manual/ Power operated/ Robot/ All of these)
All of these

42. Many of the Coconut Post Harvest Machineries were developed at? (CICR, Nagpur/ CPCRI, Kasaragod/ IISR, Bengaluru/ CIAE RC, Coimbatore)
CPCRI, Kasaragod

43. Generally how many types of Cutter bar Knife Section available? What are they?
Standard type 76 mm

Low cut type 38 mm

Medium type 50.8 mm

44. What are the losses involved in forage harvesting?
A. Cutting, Clipping and Shatter

B. Fermentation, Leaching

C. Bleaching losses

(A and C only/ All the three sets/ A only/ All the above)
All the three sets

45. Driver A says 'fast driving is one of the most common causes of higher combine losses'. Driver B said a refusing statement to Driver A.
(Driver A is correct and Driver B is wrong in their statements/ Driver B is correct/ Driver A is wrong/ Driver A is wrong and Driver B may or may not be correct)
Driver A is correct and Driver B is wrong in their statements.

46. Time loss due to turning is not dependent on machine's pattern of operation (Correct/ Incorrect)

Incorrect

47. Ratio of theoretical operating time to theoretical time plus time losses caused by the use of the pattern is referred as (Field efficiency/ Field capacity/ Implement efficiency/ Pattern efficiency)

Pattern efficiency

48. Pattern efficiency = (Furrow ploughing time/Total ploughing time)

Total time = (Furrow ploughing time + Turning time + Dead furrow finishing time)

(Both the equations are correct and relatable/ No relation between the equations/ Both are incorrect/ Second statement only holds good)

Both the equations are correct and relatable

49. Give three different types of capacities for a farm machine?
    i.   *Field capacity*

    ii. *Material capacity*

    iii. *Throughput capacity*

50. Pick a exclusive sugarcane machine from the following set (Picker/ Rotovator/ Detrasher/ Climber)

Detrasher

51. Coconut climbers are available commercially in the modes of (Manual/ Power/ Hoist/ All of these)

All of these

52. What is the necessity for research and development on mini combine harvesters?

53. What are the applications of a spading machine?

54. List out the different metering mechanisms for urea.

55. Infer about the idea of attaching ground wheels to brush cutter, auger digger and cono weeder.

56. Combine harvester's driver cabin was at more height and opaque to the rear view mostly. Formulate a simple low cost equipment to avoid human injuries/deaths due to the above fact.

57. A hill farmer Prabha has 10 acre of land with mono cropping. When Engineer Akila approached her with an innovative idea of mechanizing the cultivation process of the Prabha's field. Referring to the weight of the machinery described by Akila, Prabha denied as the machinery may compact the soil. Now suggest suitable measures to Akila for convincing Prabha in the view of eliminating soil compaction in Prabha's hill farm.

58. Vikram wants to mechanize his carrot field. Suggest a package of machinery for smart carrot cultivation with commercial availability.

59. Formulate a concept for tree shaking machine applied on a common tree prevalent all over India.

60. If a farmer Boopathi approaches you with a problem of replacing his rotovator blades. He has brought a sample blade. Now you have to direct Boopathi to a right vendor with right specifications. How will you approach this situation?

61. Adharsh has marginal area of farm holding, but he is willing to mechanize his farm completely. He has an opportunity to utilize a 35 hp powered tractor from his nephew by spending

running charges alone. But, his field requires at least 4 different implements or attachments. Assume that you are a government employee for policy frameworks in agricultural mechanization, what suggestion you will make and to whom (farmer/custom hire vendors/government) based on the above situation?

62. Assume that you are a farm machinery designer/developer in a private firm. A peculiar problem was assigned to you. The task was to design and develop a machine suitable for harvesting crop in flooded condition. The flood may raised due to sudden disaster or heavy rains. Give a short outline of idea to attend this problem.

63. Pravitha was a curry leaf grower and had a problem with timely harvest due to labour shortage. Now, if she wants to mechanize the harvest operation, what are the initial assessments (on crops) required for designing a curry leaf harvest machine?

64. Give the factors influencing the performance and power requirement of a self propelled weeder

65. Sreehari was a large land holding farmer with monocropping, and approaches sales manager Suraja to purchase a brush cutter. Whether Suraja can assist him to buy brushcutter straight-away?

66. Give the advantages of battery/solar powered knapsack sprayer over engine powered knapsack sprayer.

67. A. Shovel type openers are best suited for stony or root infested fields

    B. Shoe Type works well in trashy soils

    (A and B are correct/ A and B are incorrect/ A and B are not used together/ Both a and b are correct)

    Both a and b are correct

68. Combine harvesters' adjustment play an important role in rice harvesting. The ability of the operator plays an important role in rice harvesting.

    (Both the statements are correct/ Both the statements are wrong/ One is correct and other is wrong/ None of the above)

    Both the statements are correct

CHAPTER 4

INDUSTRY PERSPECTIVES

1. There are more than 20 registered drone manufactures and importers in India. (True/False)

   True

2. Name the models of drones mainly used for agriculture.

   Omni Agri 01 and Agribot UAV

3. First Drone company to avail Agricultural Drone Subsidy from the government is?

   Garuda Aerospace

4. Name the power sprayer manufacturing companies and its headquarters

   ASPEE - Mumbai

   Kisankraft - Bengaluru

   Mahindra Boom sprayers - Mumbai (head office)

5. Captain tractors headquarters in India is located at?

   Rajkot, Gujarat

6. Where is MTR, Agricultural Engineering related industry?

   Bengaluru

7. What is the expansion for TVS, the automobile company?

   Thirukkurungudi Vengaram Sundaram

8. In which year, first CNG tractor was introduced in India after six months of trial by a joint venture?

2021

9. When first tractor introduced in India, Eicher allied with company which undertakes distribution, service of tractors in India. Name of the company?

Good Earth

10. TAFE developed a planter for the crop?

Potato

11. Where is 'Kartar' company headquartered?

Patiala, Punjab

12. Which is the world largest tractor?

Big bud 747

13. Which is India's leading tractor manufacturer?

Mahindra & Mahindra

14. Expand AMMA

Agricultural Machineries Manufacturers Association

15. World's leading tractor company?

John Deere

16. Which tractor holds the tractor stroke length to be same for all capacity?

John Deere

17. What may be the cost of driverless tractors yet to be commercialized?

18. Where is the John Deere head quartered in India?

Pune

19. Which are the famous power tiller companies in South India?

    VST, KAMCO

20. Where is the 'Redlands' company headquarters and factory located?

    Head office - Thrissur

    Factory - Malumichampatti, Coimbatore

21. What is Boston Dynamics?

    American engineering and robotics design company

22. Lakshmi Envirotech is the manufacturer of?

    Baler

23. Redland is a company manufacturing what famous machinery?

    Transplanter, Baler

24. Which are the Industries manufacturing Combine harvesters in India?

    Class, Kartar, Ace, John Deere

25. Kirloskar is an industry, manufacturing what products and where the headquarters is located in India?

    Oil engines, Generators, Power tillers

    Pune

26. Swaraj is the division of which tractor company?

    Mahindra & Mahindra

27. Some of the engine makes used in Indian Agricultural machineries

    Honda, Mitsubishi, Simpson etc

28. Expansion of TAFE and where it is headquartered?

    Tractor and Farm Equipments, Chennai

29. Name some thresher manufacturer in South India

    Kovai classic industries,

    Valasumani,

    Standard

30. Name a company manufacturing Power operated Coconut Dehusker in India.

31. TAFE is in collaboration with?

    Massey Ferguson

    AGCO

    (TAFE was the India's licensee for Massey ferguson

    TAFE has collaboration with AGCO

    TAFE bought Eicher industries in 2005

    TAFE exports to 100 around countries)

32. What is the Expansion for KAMCO?

    Kerala Agro Machinery Corporation (Government of Kerala Undertaking)

33. Where is the headquarters of Shaktiman Agro equipment?

    Rajkot, Gujarat

34. Where is the world headquarter of John deere?

    Illinois, USA

35. Which Tractor Company has launched Electric tractor in India by 2020?

36. Name the tractor company offered free ploughing in some Indian states during the COVID-19 lockdown periods in 2020.

    TAFE – MF

37. What is MNC? Name few tractor companies under the term MNC.

Multi National Corporations,

➢ *John Deere*

➢ *Mahindra & Mahindra*

➢ *Sonalika*

38. AutoTrac is the feature of? (John Deere/ Kovai Classic Industries/ CNH Industrial/ Bosch)

John Deere

39. See and Spray technology was launched by the company?

John Deere

40. DJI is a renowned drone manufacturer. What does DJI stands for?

Da-Jiang Innovations

41. Nissan is a company introduced robot called 'Duck' for the purpose of? (Harvesting/ Pest weed clearing/ Drying/ Entertainment)

Pest weed clearing

Table: Important Agricultural Machineries Manufacturing Clusters/Industries/Concentrations Locations in 4 Different Zones of Indian Subcontinent

S. No	Zone	Locations
1	South	Coimbatore, Palakkadu, Salem, Chennai, Madurai, Ernakulam, Kochi, Bangalore, Anantapur, Kakinada, Guntur, Hyderabad
2	East	Bhubaneshwar, Calcutta, Sambhalpur, Durgapur, Patna, Ranchi, Vardhaman, Dhanbad, Muzaffarpur
3	West	Anand, Bombay, Pune, Sangli, Vidisha, Gwalior, Kohlapur, Sholapur, Ahmedabad, Nagpur, Khurai, Raipur, Junagarh, Bhopal, Indore, Baroda, Dewas, Bina
4	North	Ludhiana, Meeratpur, Karnal, Panipat, Lucknow, Kanpur, Faridabad, Delhi, Agra, Moga, Jalandhar, Batala, Rudrapur, Goraya, Meerut, Fatehpur, Allahabad, Ghaziabad, Hoshiyarpur

42. **Match the following**

S. No.	A	M. No.	B
1	Massey Ferguson	a	Chennai
2	John Deere	b	Hary Ferguson
3	HMT	c	Oxford of the East
4	Pune	d	Bengaluru
5	TAFE	e	Steel plough
6	Mason Vaugh	f	America

Ans: 1-b, 2-e, 3-d, 4-c, 5-a, 6-f

43. **Match the following**

S. No.	A	M. No.	B
1	CLAAS	a	Rotary tiller & Paddy Master
2	John Deere	b	Rotary tiller & Baler
3	Shaktiman	c	Brush cutters
4	Redlands	d	Super seeder & MAT unit
5	Honda	e	Chandigarh
6	Gomathi	f	Balers

Ans: 1-e, 2-d, 3-a, 4-f, 5-c, 6-b

44. Cotton Master was a product of company headquartered at Rajkot. Name the company.

Shaktiman

45. Honda, Stihl, Kisankraft were commonly known brush cutter manufacturers in India. (True/False)

True

46. Bull is a leading Indian manufacturer of backhoes and loaders (True/False)

False

47. AMMA-India was established in the year 2010. What is AMMA?

All-India Agricultural Machinery Manufacturers' Association

48. (a) Green – TAFE, (b) Blue – Sonalika, (c) Yellow – M&M, (d) Red – John Deere. Identify the correct pairs. (All are correct/None was correct/Partially correct/None of the above)

Partially correct

49. What is meant by phantom?

A. Series of UAV developed by DJI,

B. Jet fighter aircraft introduced in 1947

C. Apparition

Scholar from Institution A says that option A was correct answer. But scholar from Institution B denies that and said all are correct. Scholar from Institution C judged that scholar Institution A was correct and scholar from institution B is completely wrong even speaking in general. These are the three different views of three scholars from institutions A, B and C. If the view of a scholar was correct, then the institution will get a score of 5 or else stays zero. Score of institution C will be (10/5/0/15)

0

50. Apollo, Good Year, JK is a group with one missing member. Find out the member from the following options (JD/AIMS/M&M/ MRF)
MRF

51. Mahindra Research Valley is a NABL accredited facility (Yes/No)
Yes

52. A well-known tractor manufacturer is partnering with a luxury car company to design the front appearance of their tractors. Interpret this statement for practical happenings.

53. 'Nothing runs like a Deere' belongs to (JD/M&M/SDF/All the above
JD

54. DUMS is a manufacturer of (Tractor/Power tiller/Combine harvester/Drone)
Drone

55. CLAAS is an agricultural machinery manufacturer not based in Germany (Correct/Partially correct/Wrong/None)

Partially correct

56. AIAMMA was/will be established in the year (2000/2010/ 2020/2030)

2010

57. In terms of spare parts, what is the expansion of OE? Aysha said OE stands for Operable Equipment. But Praveen said it was Original Engine shortened to OE. Kiruthiga has to find out the right answer. She answered correctly by observing Aysha and Praveen's answers. How?

58. Siva is attending an interview in the tractor company. Basically, Siva has financial problems with his life and requires an immediate professional job. HR Sanjeev has raised two questions as follows.

    a. Why we should hire you?

    b. How many days you are planning to be in this position?

    What should be the Siva's answer for the above two questions?

59. During an interview, drone company hirer asks you - Where do you see yourself in five years? What will be your answer?

60. When Janani was an Assistant manager at a farm implement manufacturing company, her senior manager made a deadline on the day, and conveyed that he couldn't be reachable for the whole day. On the same day, a farmer approached her for a post sales service, where she was the only expert available in the company to the service. If the service is denied or postponed, a huge loss will be imposed to the farmer. Now Janani has to

decide to do either senior manager's task or farmer service. What will be your decision if you are at Janani's position?

61. If you are at an interview, a question that 'what is the special skill with you for which we can hire you?' was raised by HR. What would be your answer if it is a farm implement manufacturing company?

62. What is the difference between,

    a. Oral test and interview

    b. Entrepreneur and businessman

    c. Resume and curriculum vitae

63. The phrase "sales and marketing" is often used together. Why?

64. Skill set requirement for sales professional and marketing professional are same or different? If yes, what are the differences?

65. When HR asked Antony, whether it is possible to stop using AI tools like ChatGPT for a day and complete the task in the same time frame, what thoughtful reply can Antony give?

66. Effective teamwork is crucial for achieving common goals in any organization. Similarly for working in a tractor company, select the quality does not apply for a team work.

    A. Active Listening B. Flexibility C. Diversity Appreciation D. Surface-Level Thinking.

    (A and D/ D only/ C and D/ C only)

67. If you are an entrepreneur and at a stage of hiring an engineering graduate. The position is to design making in computer. Whether you will prefer fresher or experienced?

68. What do you consider to be your greatest strength and your greatest weakness in the field of farm mechanization?

69. What is the most important skill required for the common employee, when the company has frequent changes in locality/ workstation? (Adaptability/ Team work/ Qualification/ Ethics)
Adaptability

70. Does confidentiality is the aspect of industrial ethics? (Yes/No)
Yes

CHAPTER 5

ERGONOMICS AND SAFETY

1. The main objective of Ergonomics is?
To design

2. According to Indian rules/standards how many persons can sit in a tractor?
One

3. Expansion for CMVR?
Central Motor Vehicle Rule

4. Frequency range for human ears is 16 Hz to 20000 Hz. (Lower limit is wrong/ both are wrong/ Nothing wrong)?
Nothing Wrong

5. Drone pilot must not consume alcohol for how many hours prior to flying?
Eight hours

6. Drones must not fly over a private properties or gathering of people without permission. (True/False)
True

7. Practically, an adult can perceive sound above?
11000 Hz

8. What is the average surface area of human?
2.0 sq.mt (ICAR hand book on Agricultural Engineering)
1.8 sq.mt (Martin Helander, Ergonomics textbook)

9. What is meant by safety neutral switch?

    Starting Safety provision – When vehicle is not in the neutral position, the switch prevents the driver to start the engine

10. What are the emission norms in India for tractors and trucks?

    Tractors – BS III A

    Trucks – BS VI, BS VI (BS IV vehicle registrations up to April 2020 only).

11. If future is Artificial Intelligence, Manless Agriculture, and Mechatronics world, then the role of Ergonomics will...(Increase/ Applied to human fingers alone/ Drops drastically/ Becomes zero)

12. Predominant tractor vibration is in vertical direction. (True/ False)?

    True

13. Why Cab Pressurization essential?

    To prevent dust entry

14. Cab pressurization in the range of 50 – 100 Pa above outside pressure is? (Too high/ Feasible/ Not at all sufficient)

15. What may be the normal walking speed of a human?

    0.7 to 0.8 m/s

16. What is electromyography?

    Evaluating and recording the electrical activity produced by skeletal muscles. Term used in analysis of biomechanics of human or animal movement.

17. (A) There are real indications that either operator age or experience gave increased performance. (B) The statement was

wrong and truth is there are no such indications. (B) is (True/False/Complete)

True

18. Lower limit of bearable zone of humidity is 30% (True/False)

    True

19. In a agricultural machine, following safety devices may present. Identify them

    A.   Automatic intermittent horn while reversing

    B.   Indicator lights

    C.   Stone traps

    D.   Spark arrester

    E.   Shear pin

    F.   Slip clutches

    G.   Bevameter

    H.   Fall army worm gear

    (A to G/A to H/B to F/A to F)

    A to F

20. Name an agricultural machine mentioned as dangerous as per dangerous machines act.

    Power thresher

21. In a rearward overturning of a tractor with ROPS, the first hit part on the ground is normally the (Upper and side edges/Upper edge/Upper and lower edges/Rear edge)

    Upper edge

22. Mention some of the types of tractor accidents causing fatalities.

    Overturning, overrun, caught in PTO

23. Permissible exposure of noise levels

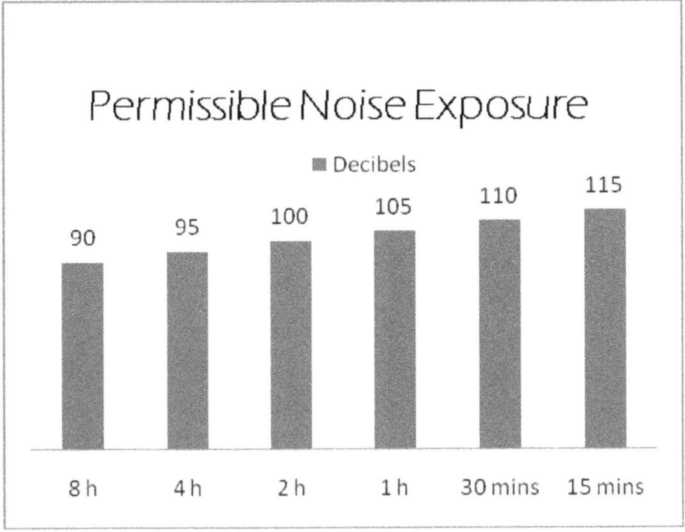

Durations per day (X axis) and Sound level in Decibels (Y axis)

24. **Match the following**

S. No.	A	M. No.	B
1	Scales	**a**	Actuations
2	Push pull tester	**b**	Knapsack power sprayer
3	Surface thermometer	**c**	Trolleys
4	Parking brake	**d**	Dimensions
5	Main and parking brakes	**e**	Hot parts
6	Quick release clutch	**f**	Self propelled machines

Ans: 1-f, 2-c, 3-a, 4-e, 5-d, 6-b

25. Shape of SMV emblem is (Rectangle/Spheroid/Triangle/None)
Triangle

26. Match the following

S. No.	A	M. No.	B
1	Wearing a seat belt	a	Entanglements
2	Guard	b	8
3	Unique Identification Number	c	ROPS
4	No alcoholic drinks	d	DGCA

Ans: 1-c, 2-a, 3-d, 4-b

27. Central Insecticides Board and Registration Committee (CIB&RC) approved Pesticides or Insecticides cannot be used (True/False)

False

28. ASAE recommendations include:

   d. Four head lights.

   c. At least one tail lamp, mounted on the left side facing the rear of the tractor.

   b. At least two amber warning lights, visible from front and rear, mounted at the same level at least 42 inches above ground level.

   a. At least two green reflectors, visible from the rear and mounted on either side

   The above statement set contains error (True/False). If true, rearrange the sentences in   order.

   False

29. ATIN denotes (Agricultural Tractor Identification Number/ Agricultural Tractor Inventory Number/ Agricultural Tyre

Identification Number/ Agricultural Tractor Identification Night)

Agricultural Tractor Identification Number

30. Match the following

S. No.	A	M. No.	B
1	Reynaud's	a	Hand vibration
2	Dart	b	Shift
3	Dosimeter	c	Vibration
4	Chain saws	d	Vibration
5	Cardiovascular Disease	e	Noise

Ans: 1-c, 1-d, 2-c, 2-d, 3-e, 4-a, 5-e

31. Squatting - lifting, lifting index - estimate of the hazard. Whether both are paired correctly (Yes/No)

Yes

32. What are the major types of hearing losses?

Conductive hearing loss and Neural hearing loss.

33. Differentiate ear plugs and ear muffs.

34. What is GSR?

Galvanic Skin Response - measure of the electrical conductivity of a particular type of sweat gland

35. Expand PNC and PSIL.

Preferred Noise Criteria (PNC) curves

Preferred Speech Interference Level

36. Seatback angle greater than 110° can reduce the pressure on the spine (True/False)

True

37. Anthropometric data is not subjected to

    1. Interindividual variations

    2. Intraindividual variations

    3. Secular changes

    4. Poor data

    5. None

    6. 1 to 4 is correct

    5 is correct

38. A. Too high tables

    B. Glare on the screen

    C. Too low chairs

    (A and C are correct and belongs to tractor workstation/ All are correct and not   related to computer workstation/ Related to computer workstation/B is correct and   r e l e v a n t to computer workstation)

    Related to computer workstation

39. Farmer A sprays insecticide in his field using a power knapsack sprayer. Farmer B sprays same insecticide but with drone. Bystanders are different for each field. Ergonomic Scientist X says that "Bystanders at field of farmer B have less harm comparing the bystanders of farmer A field. Crop Protection Scientist Y agrees with X scientist.

    (Action of scientist Y is correct/ Statement of scientist X is error/ Drones can carry 2 persons only/All are correct)

    Action of scientist Y is correct

40. A. Type of Tractor B. CMVR type-approval Certification number C. Name of the manufacturer. Rearrange in order. (BAC, CBA, ABC, CAB)

    CAB

41. A. Influence of daylight is an vital factor in circadian rhythms B. There is no possibility of shift of the circadian cycle disturbing the digestive functions

    (A and B are correct/If A is correct, B also correct/B is wrong/A is wrong)

    B is wrong

42. Tri-axial seat accelerometer is a special purpose instrument used to measure (Acceleration/Torque/Height/Vibration)

    Vibrations

43. Expand HTV and WBV.

    Hand Transmitted Vibration (HTV) and Whole Body Vibration (WBV)

44. A. The human body is not symmetrical B. Response to a vibration is based upon the direction of vibration application. (A and B are correct and irrelevant/A and B are relevant/Both are error statements/A is not correct but B is correct)

    A and B are relevant

45. Manufacturer's plate shall not be mandatory for all Agricultural Tractors. The statement is (Correct/Incorrect)

    Incorrect

46. In tool design guidelines, find the optimum values for the following - Grip thickness (mm), Grip length minimum (mm), Tool weight maximum (kg)

(400, 10, 100/ 8–13, 100, 1.75 /13, 100, 0.01/ 10, 1000, 2)

8–13, 100, 1.75

47. The lifting index (LI) provides a simple estimate of the hazard of an overexertion injury for a manual lifting job. (True/False)

True

48. Match the following

S. No.	A	M. No.	B
1	Visible light	a	180 to 380
2	Laser scanning	b	206
3	Bones	c	380 to 760
4	UV	d	3D

Ans: 1-c, 2-d, 3-b, 4-a

49. **Match the following**

S. No.	A	M. No.	B
1	CVD	a	Meeting
2	Exoskeleton	b	Support
3	Disruption of social life	c	Epilepsy
4	Brain	d	Shift workers

Ans: 1-d, 2-b, 3-a, 4-c

50. **Match the following**

S. No.	A	M. No.	B
1	Joints	a	Movement
2	Resonance	b	Degrees of freedom
3	Kinesiology	c	WBV
4	Tractor operator	d	Vibration

Ans: 1-b, 2-d, 3-c, 4-c

51. Identify the differences between user centred design and human centred design

52. What are the applications of Exoskeletons in Agriculture?

53. Do you have any idea on 'Cyborgs'?

54. **Match the following**

S. No.	A	M. No.	B
1	Lighting	**a**	Manual Handling
2	Cycle Time	**b**	Work Environment
3	Grip Strength	**c**	Repetitive Movements
4	Bending	**d**	Work Posture

Ans: 1-b, 2-c, 3-a, 4-d

55. Name some ergo refined equipments or tools in agriculture.

56. Drone spraying affects the pilot and co-pilot with drift borne chemical hazard. What are the protective measures to be carried out?

57. Differences between

1. Macro ergonomics and micro ergonomics

2. Ergonomic risk assessment and ergonomic evaluation

3. Anthropometrics and biomechanics

4. Static and dynamic ergonomics

5. Safety audit and safety inspection

6. Incident and accident

7. Confined space and restricted space

8. Hazard and risk

9. Privacy and security

10. Posture and positioning

58. Give an innovative idea to combat the drudgery experienced by paddy farmers on fertilizer application in a wetland.

59. Extremely heavy work - 150-170. What does the 150-170 refers to? (Lux/ Heart rate/ Glucose level/ Blood pressure)
Heart rate

60. For a safer operation of chaff cutters, select the correct sets from the below,
    1. Avoid feeding ear-heads with stalks
    2. Near the threshing yard, do not smoke or light a fire
    3. Use only those threshers, which are fitted with safe feeding chute as per BIS standards

    (1 and 3/ 1, 2 and 3/ 3 only/ 2 and 3)
    2 and 3

61. Why the horn buttons are present on the left side of the steering?

62. Differentiate bearable zone and comfort zone of different environmental parameters.

63. Upto your knowledge, which of the farm operation may have high dust concentrations?

64. What is the role of back rests when foot operated activities are crucial in a self-propelled machine?

65. Why the accelerator pedal exerts less force from the foot comparing the brake pedals?

66. Peak pressure under the ischial tuberosities should be limited to X g/cm^2. The value of X may be (9/90/900/9000)
    90

67. Operator not necessarily use a seat belt when operating tractor fitted with ROPS. (True/False)
    False

68. SPL is expressed in (dB/cB/fb/tB)

    dB

69. Noise generating components in tractor engine are

    1. Engine exhausts, bearings, piston slap

    2. Gears, Valve train

    3. Battery, tyne, ROPS

    (1 and 3 only/ 3 is incorrect/ 2 is correct/ Both B and C)

    Both B and C

70. Biggest sources of noise are (Combustion and Piston slap/ Battery and Combustion/ Valve train and Combustion/ Bearings and Combustion)

    Combustion and Piston slap

71. What are the essential ergonomical requirements for a power tiller operated in a hill farm? Enumerate.

72. What do you understand about the term Work-Life Balance?

73. What are the key ergonomic aspects for a computer workstation refinement? Assume that station is used for image procession.

74. Suggest the ergonomic measures suitable for the following situations.

    Situation 1: An unexpected fault occurred on the tractor while operating a heavy implement in a complex field situation

    Situation 2: A new or different machine was imposed on a operator at a critical situation

75. Mention some stress reduction features as psychological support for a tractor driver.

CHAPTER 6
TESTING

1. What are the four testing institutes for Farm Machinery in India? Among all 4 testing centers, which is famous for what testing?

   Budhni (Madhya Pradesh) – Tractor

   Hisar (Haryana) – Combine

   Bishwanath chariali (Assam) – Implements

   Anantapur (Andhra Pradesh) – Power tillers

2. What is the maximum limit (%) of variation in seed discharge due to different forward speeds? (8/9/10/15)

   15

3. What is the maximum limit (%) of variation in seed discharge due to box filling? (8/9/10/15)

   10

   A. Engine performance test is conducted for self propelled combines also

   B. Engine performance test is conducted for self propelled combines only

   C. Engine performance test is not conducted for self propelled combines only

   D. Engine performance test is conducted for self propelled combines rarely

Statement A & D regarding engine performance test are correct (True/False)

False

4. If Bosch value exceeds 5, it is unacceptable in case of?

5. (Fuel efficiency/Hydraulic pressure/Smoke intensity/Combine output)

Smoke intensity

6. In combines, endurance test is carried out for a period (mins) of (60/250/6000/15000)

15000

7. In combines, normally rated specific fuel consumption is g/bhp/hr is? (0 to 169/170 to 200/201 to 225/226 and above)

170 to 200

8. Identify the suitable options. In combines, critical component(s) is/are

A. Peg tooth & rasp bar

B. Ledger plate and knife section

C. Knife guard

D. Knife guard and Peg tooth

(A&B only/ A,B,C&D/A and D only/A,B & D)

A,B,C&D

9. What is the minimum Standing angle of crops required for combine harvester testing?

60 deg

10. Where First tractor testing held?

Omaha, Nebraska

11. What is NTTL?

    Nebraska Tractor Testing Laboratory

12. Which is the first established testing centre in India? (Bhopal/ Garlandine/Bhopal/Hisar)

    Budhni

13. Ministry governing all testing institutes for Farm machinery in India?

    Ministry of Agriculture and Farmers Welfare

14. SAU testing centers can test engines upto the power of 5 hp (True/False)

    True

15. Tractors can be tested in SAU testing centers also from 25.12.2019. (True/ False)

    False

16. What is endurance test?

17. A duster confirms a test when there is not more than 0.5% of input dust remains in the hopper (True/False)

    True

18. Dusters are tested for ability to throw dusts upto 40 inches in approximate (True/False/Neither true nor False/May be true)

    True

19. Strap drop test for dusters are conducted at X height (mm) and repeated for Y times. The X & (Y+5) are (300 & 300/300 & 305/300 & 30/30 & 300)

    300 & 30

20. What are parameters in testing quality of work?

21. Noise measurement to be done at (Bystander's position/Operator's hand level/Operator's ear level/Both A and C)

    Both A and C

22. What are the measures of agricultural machine performance?

    Rate (Quantity per time) and quality of operation

23. Test engineer A says, Von brand smoke meter can give intermittent reading of smoke intensity. But Test engineer B denies his statement with his knowledge. Knowledge of Test Engineer B is (Poor/Nil/Good/None of the above)

    Good

24. (A) Soil inversion characteristics can be measured by weed count method (B) Soil inversion is expressed in kg/cm^2 (A and B are true/B is true/A is false/B is false)

    B is false

25. Mention the high ambient temperature for PTO testing. $(45°/25°/35°/0°)$

    45°

26. Mention a most popular smoke meter (Roast/Fergusson/Bosch/Sandra)

    Bosch

27. Total missing hills includes (Floating hills/Buried hills/missing hills/all of the above)

    All of the above

28. Suggested missing hills (%) must be less than (100/10/1000/1)

    10

29. Test plot of transplanting machine testing should have a dimension (Length in cm & Width in cm) of? (250 & 500/100 & 250/500 & 250/500 & 100)

    500 & 250

30. Identify the correct statement. 15 h testing time to be adopted for

    A. Tractor performance with wetland

    B. Tractor performance with cultivator

    C. Transplanter water proof testing

    D. Depth of cut identification in mowers

    Statement C is correct

31. The term 'square corners' associated with turning radius. (B) Square corners are permitted by the cutter bar mowers having short enough turning radius. (Both statements are true/ A is true B is false/ Both are false/All the above)

    Both the statements are true

32. **Match the following**

S. No.	A	M. No.	B
1	Tarmacadam	a	2%
2	Mown	b	Cold, hot, hand
3	Belt slip	c	Steel wheeled tractor
4	Turning ability test	d	Carbon density
5	Smoke meters	e	1.5 to 2 kmph tractor speed
6	Brake tests	f	Pneumatic tyre tractors

   Ans: 1-f, 2-c, 3-a, 4-e, 5-d, 6-b

33. Match the following

S. No.	A	M. No.	B
1	75 kg	a	Vibration meter
2	400 N	b	Brake test
3	Microns	c	Water proof test
4	Highest forward speed	d	Set weight of the operator
5	6 kmph (apxmt.)	e	Noise level
6	ILO	f	Hand brake lever

Ans: 1-d, 2-f, 3-a, 4-b, 5-c, 6-e

34. Match the following

S. No.	A	M. No.	B
1	Field efficiency	a	Quality of work
2	Depth of cut	b	2:1
3	Test plot	c	Average of 5 runs
4	Width of cut	d	Average of 10 places
5	Soil inversion	e	Rate of work
6	Soil pulverization	f	Average of 5 places

Ans: 1-e, 2-d, 3-b, 4-c, 5-f, 6-a

35. Match the following

S. No.	A	M. No.	B
1	Sieving	a	Smoke measurement
2	Weed count	b	Soil pulverization
3	Carbon density	c	Soil inversion
4	Dynamometer	d	Evenness of seed spacing
5	Sticky belt	e	Draft measurement

Ans: 1-b, 2-c, 3-a, 4-e, 5-d

36. Wear analysis for barpoint will be done after 1500 minutes (True/False)

    True

    A. Hardness of share, barpoint etc is observed for a disc plough

    B. Chemical composition can be analysed using SPECTRA PLUS MULTI CD SPECTROMETER

    (i.Both A and B are correct/ii.A is wong/iii.B is correct/iv.Both i and ii are correct)

    Both i and ii are correct

37. A. Manufacturer's address B. Model C. Specific fuel consumption D. Engine serial No.

    Above data may be provided on the (Labelling plate/Engine front casing/Tyre side/Seating)

    Labelling plate

38. Noise measurement is done at (Bystanders position/Implement hitch point/Farm office mate/Tractor co-rider)

    Bystanders position

39. Deviation observed in a spring test of sprayer manufacturer A more than 20%

    Deviation observed in a spring test of sprayer manufacturer B doesn't exceed 20%

    Deviation observed in a spring test of sprayer manufacturer C is 6%

    Deviation observed in a spring test of sprayer manufacturer D is 4%

    (sprayer manufacturer qualifying the testing was (A/B/C/D)

    D

40. Number of repetition of dropping in a strap test of a power sprayer is (5/25/24/23)

    24

41. Gasket test, Spring test, strap test are subjected to (balers/sprayers/weeders/drones)

    Sprayers

42. Applicant comments cannot take part on test report (True/False)

    False

43. A. Number of operators required for operating the tested machine will be noted down.

    B. Also the countries were the machine was in commercial use will be listed out.

    Scientist A had informed an Engineer X to check A and B for making a test report on farm machinery. Engineer X checked A and skipped B. Action of Engineer X is

    (Not fulfilled for a test report/Satisfactory for a test report/None of the above/Scientist A is perfectly correct on the requirements)

    Satisfactory for a test report

44. For speed measurement, number of poles suggested for experimentation is (1/5/4/20)

    4

45. Blade, Skid, Adjusting Rack, Hitch Pyramid, Mast, PTO Drive Shaft were tested for a (Power tiller engine/Rotovator/Front mounted reaper/Splendor plus)

    Rotovator

46. Dynamometer is associated with (Draft measurement/Puddling index/Tractor idling/None of the above)

    Draft measurement

47. Ratio between settled soil volume and excess water volume is referred as Puddling index. (True/False)

    False

48. A. Core sampling is done for a bulk density measurement

    B. The samples are taken upto 10 cm below the working tillage depth

    (A and B are correct and irrelevant/A is correct, B is wrong/B is correct and relevant to   A/ is incorrect)

    B is correct and relevant to A

49. Duration of field test for pumps should be not be less than 60 minutes (True/False/Both/None)

    True

50. Give a list of instruments/equipments important for a drone testing laboratory establishment in an Institute.

51. Infer about climate controlled testing laboratories and their needs in future agricultural machinery testing

52. Give a test procedure for assessing the accuracy and precision of a GPS device.

53. Discuss with your classmate/senior regarding the applications of automation and IoT in farm machinery testing

54. Explain the structural requirement for a soil bin establishment.

55. Differentiate between consistency and compliance.

56. Find the odd one out (NABL/BIS/ARAI/IEI)

    IEI

57. What do you know about the propeller (wind mill and/or drone) testing?

58. Enumerate about wind tunnels and thrust stand.

59. How to test a solar PV module to be used in a agricultural machine working in a dusty environment?

60. Name a test applied for testing newly developed chulah.

61. Non-Destructive Testing – give an overview.

62. Defect identification was the only major reason for testing any machine (True/False)

    False

63. Assume any agricultural machine which is familiar to you. By understanding the test procedures available, find out the drawback or 'test gap' (a necessary testing which might left out or ignored in the existing procedure) for enhanced reliability of the machine.

64. What are the major responsibilities of a test engineer in a farm machinery testing centre?

65. In farm machinery testing terms, cutter bar losses accounts to (Rate of work/Quality of work/Rate of produce/Quality of produce)

    Quality of work

CHAPTER 7

ENERGY MANAGEMENT

1. Density of Hydrogen is? (0.08988 L/g / 0 g/L / 0.08988 g/L / C is wrong)

   0.08988 g/L

2. Scholar A written an sentence, "Air has less density than Hydrogen". Scholar B read the sentence and stated Scholar A's sentence is wrong. The statement of Scholar B is (Correct/ Wrong)?

   Correct

3. What is KREDL in Karnataka?

   Karnataka Renewable Energy Development Limited

4. What is $SCCO_2$? What role does it can have in Energy sector?

   Supercritical carbon dioxide, its high density and compressibility would enable generators to extract more power from turbines.

5. Plastic waste can be converted into Pyrolytic oil. (True/False)

   True

6. Animal energy is highly versatile source of energy. Contribution of such energy is in what kind of trend in the farming activities?

   Declining trend

7. What is energy productivity?

   Yield produced per Unit of Energy input (eg. Kg/MJ)

8. The ratio between the energy developed and consumed by a system is called as? (Efficiency/Energy Estimation/Energy Give Out Ratio (EGR)/Energy Payback Ratio (EPR))
   Energy Payback Ratio (EPR)

9. What is meant by the net energy gain from Agricultural production process?
   Gross energy production – Total energy input

10. What are the Possible Renewable fuels for tractor?
    Fuel cells, Biogas, Biodiesel, Electricity from Renewable Sources

11. By treating e-waste properly, what renewable fuel can be generated?
    Hydrogen

12. What is the expansion for BEE? (Bureau of Energy Estimation/ Board of Energy Efficiency/ Bureau of Energy Efficiency/Board of Elite Efficiency)
    Bureau of Energy Efficiency

13. What is the full form for MNRE?
    Ministry of New and Renewable Energy sources

14. What is meant by energy ratio in Agriculture?
    Ratio of caloric value of output products to the energy sequestered in production process

15. What is the target set for renewable energy in 2022 and 2030 by India?
    175 and 500 GW

16. In a combustion chamber/furnace, if excess air is supplied without oxygen, the combustion efficiency will increases

(Absolutely True/ Partly True/ True in the case of engine alone/ False/ Varies according to location)

False

17. A. Non powered implements require less energy than powered ones,

   B. Non powered implements require more field operations for obtaining the same size of aggregates

   (A and B are incorrect and relatable/ A and B are correct and relatable/A is correct and B is wrong, not relatable/None)

   A and B are correct and relatable

18. For primary tillage, moldboard plowing requires ______ than chiseling (less energy/ more energy/ equal depth/ more depth)

   more energy

19. Wheel slip reduction (6%–7%), drawbar power increase (10%–12%), and fuel savings (up to 20%) can be achieved in tractors when,

   Radial tires at low inflation pressures are used instead of bias tires

20. Power-shift transmissions save energy (Correct/ Incorrect/ Irrelevant to energy/False)

   Correct

21. Overall energy involved in fertilizer includes

   A. Production B.Transportation C.Application, D.Packaging

   (A, B & D are correct/A & D are correct/ B, D, A, & C are correct/B, C & D are correct)

   B, D, A, and C are correct

22. A. Chemical fertilizers are widely used in agricultural crops

   B. Require high rates of direct energy for their production,

C. The above 2 statement mainly focus nitrogen fertilizer industry,

D. High energy content incorporated during manufacturing and ability to be lost quickly

(A and B are correct, but D is not explanation to C/ C and B are incorrect, but D is an explanation to C/ A, B and C are correct, but D is an explanation to C/ A and C are   incorrect, but D is not explanation to C)

A, B and C are correct, but D is an explanation to C

23. To save energy in transportation – Proper maintenance, Good driving habits, Good planning on reduce trips and selection of the most economical vehicles can be done (Incorrect/Correct)
Correct

24. Average power output of Human in manual operation will be (0.01–0.08 W/0.01–0.08 kW/0.01–0.08 MJ/0.01–0.08 BTU)
0.01–0.08 kW

25. Energy Returned on Energy Invested (EROEI) ratio is a highly useful indicator for evaluating the ________of energy sources (Quantity/Losses/Perception/Efficiency)
Efficiency

26. Loading the vehicle up to its ________ capacity reduces energy intensiveness (maximum/5 tonnes/1 ton/3 tonnes)
Maximum

27. Detecting defects, predicting energy production were the applications of Artificial Intelligence in energy sector. (Exactly Correct/Partially correct/Not at all correct/Slightly correct
Exactly Correct

28. How does directly/indirectly variable rate technology minimize the energy footprints? (Reducing chemical inputs/ Reducing transportation load/ Reducing machinery use and wear/ All the above)

    All the above

29. Differentiate renewable energy and sustainable energy

30. List out the major energy crops.

31. In a HVAC system, power consumption was increased with the same load. What may be the reason(s)?

    A. Fault in expansion valve

    B. Less gas level

    C. Not functioning of thermister

    (All three/ A and C only/ C is incorrect/ None)

    All three

32. PCRA works with policymakers to develop and implement policies related to energy conservation and efficient use of wind energy products. (True/False)

    False

33. PCRA operates under the ministry of (Agriculture/ Petroleum and Natural Gas/ New & Renewable Energy/ Energy Conservation)

    Petroleum and Natural Gas

34. What do you know about the 'manufactured embodied energy of farm machinery'?

35. Energy Conservation Act (EC Act) was enacted in (2001/1991/2011/2021)

    2001

36. Select any protected cultivation farm and assess the energy conservation possibilities.

37. BEE is under the ministry of (Industrial development/ Petroleum and Natural Gas/ New & Renewable Energy/ Power)

    Power

38. Relevant to BEE, what are mandatory labeling and voluntary labeling?

39. Smart Irrigation Technologies can be an directly/indirectly aspect of energy management (Yes/No)

    Yes

40. Study the relationship between tyres and energy efficiency

41. Why BLDC equipped fans are energy efficient?

42. The objectives of Standards & Labeling Program is to provide the consumer an informed choice about the (Energy efficiency/ Energy saving/ Energy footprint/ Energy consumption)

    Energy saving

43. Agricultural Pump Sets have (Mandatory labeling/ Voluntary labeling/ Chimney/ Lever)

    Voluntary labeling

44. A. Re use, Reuse, Recycle – Snake and Lizard

    B. Reduce, Refuse, Recycle – Lion and tiger

    C. Reduce, Reuse, Recycle – Parrot and peacock

    D. Reduce, Reuse, Repost – Dolphin and Penguin

    Select a perfect set and corresponding animal pair (Snake and Lizard/ Lion and tiger/ Parrot and peacock/ Dolphin and Penguin)

    Lion and tiger

45. Discuss about three levels if energy audit

46. Differentiate between energy auditor and energy manager

47. Give some DIY farm energy assessments.

48. Do a SWOT analysis for a solar-based water pumping system replacement of AC water pumping system.

49. How does energy management might influence the adoption of precision agriculture technologies?

50. Government subsidies can significantly influence the adoption of energy-efficient technologies (True/False)
True

51. Public charging station will comply with a tie up with at least one network service provider to enable advance online booking of charging slots by the E-vehicle holder (True/False)
True

52. Moving averages, exponential smoothing, Delphi are methods for (Energy consumed/ water flow assessment/ energy forecast/ None)
Energy forecast

53. What is energy input-output ratio?

54. Give any 5 tips for a tractor driver for conserving diesel.

55. In US, NREL stands for
National Renewable Energy Laboratory

CHAPTER 8

WIND ENERGY

1. What is meant by NIWE and where it is located?
    National Institute of Wind Energy, Chennai

2. Which is the highest wind energy producing state in India?
    (Kerala/Kolkata/Madhya Pradesh/Tamilnadu)

    Tamil Nadu

3. What is the minimum wind velocity required to operate a wind turbine?
    10 kmph or 5 mps

4. What is NACA?
    National Advisory Committee for Aeronautics

5. What is the similarity between aero plane and wind turbine?
    Aerodynamic principles

    (Wind mill blade and aero plane wings)

6. In Windmills, the blade count should be lesser or higher for water pumping? What is the expected parameter for water pumping?
    Wind mill water pumping requires multibladed rotor with high starting torque

7. What is the working principle of Bladeless windmills?
    Vortex shedding effect

8. Ministry of Agriculture and Rural Development is looking for the Offshore wind energy project in Tamilnadu and Gujarat. (True/False)

   False

9. MNRE Development is looking for the Offshore wind energy project in Tamilnadu and Gujarat. (True/False)

   True

10. In the year 2018, MNRE issues the (LIC Policy/Water Energy Nexus/Wind Solar Hybrid Policy/One lakh Solar cookers to SHGs)

    Wind Solar Hybrid Policy

11. Sonic anemometer works by senses the changes in?

    Speed of Sound in air

12. Whether Bridled anemometers and Hot wire anemometers are not common in wind energy measurements? (Correct/Incorrect)

    Correct

13. Wind Rotor blades are made of?

    Multi-layered Fiberglass, Carbon composites, Carbon-glass hybrids, and Wood

14. Savonius wind rotor blades can be arranged in a shape of a letter? (S/H/I/O)

    "S"

15. Musgrove wind rotor blades can be arranged in a shape of a letter? (S/H/I/O)

    "H"

16. Complex yaw mechanisms are required for vertical axis turbines (True/False)

    False

17. Based on direction receiving wind, horizontal axis wind turbines can be classified as?

    Upwind turbines and down wind turbines

18. Upwind turbines are better because it does not have the constraint of?

    Tower Shadow effect, More noise as downwind turbines

19. Wind energy is derivation of solar energy. Name the effect causing wind flow globally?

    Coriolis effect of wind acceleration along with temperature and density difference

20. What are the advantages of hybrid ceramic bearings?

    They are harder, stiffer, corrosion free and can sustain adverse operating conditions.

21. How offshore wind energy projects can have adverse effects on environment?

    It may affect the marine habitats due to the transportation of turbine with its components, construction of piles and other structures for the foundation, laying and burying of the cables and usage of chemicals and oils for project construction.

22. The painting of the wind rotor blades is to be in a contrasting pattern to avoid?

    Avian issues

23. What are the two types of noises from a windmill? (Mechanical/ Androgogy/Pedogogy/Aerodynamic/ Mechanical noise and Aerodynamic noise /Mechanical and Androgogic)

    Mechanical noise and Aerodynamic noise

24. Permissible Noise range varies from country to country, but the majority of the noise range of Wind rotors fixed is in the limits of?

    40 to 50 dB (A)

25. Give the difference between
    a. Air and wind
    b. Aerogenerators and aerofoil
    c. Airfoil and blade
    d. Wind Turbine and wind Generator
    e. Pitch Control and yaw Control

26. Applications of Machine learning in wind mill
    a. Energy forecasting
    b. Performance Optimization
    c. Optimal pitch control
    d. Condition Monitoring
    e. Predictive Maintenance

    (a and b are correct, c and d are not correct/ e is incorrect and others are correct/others are incorrect and e is alone correct/ none of the above)

    None of the above

27. Give the differences between
    a. Turbulence and Eddy

b.   Wind Shear and Wind Gradient

c.   Lift and drag

d.   Hover and stall

e.   Angle of Attack and Angle of Incidence

f.   Streamline and Flow Line

28. What you know about Avian Fauna Study?

29. What are the different tests for Wind Turbines
    - *Power Performance measurements*
    - *Safety & Function testing*
    - *Yaw efficiency*
    - *Load Measurements & Duration Test*
    - *Customer requested measurements tailored*

30. What is WTTS?
    Wind Turbine Test Station

31. What do you think about Wind Rose?

32. What is LCOE? (Levelized Cost of Energy/ Local Civil Operations on Energy/ Load Calculation on Energy/ Lift Coefficient of Eno)
    Levelized Cost of Energy

33. If a wind turbine experiences a sudden increase in turbulence intensity at the site, what is the most likely impact on the turbine's performance and maintenance needs?
    A.   Increased efficiency and reduced maintenance
    B.   Decreased efficiency and increased maintenance
    C.   Increased efficiency and reduced maintenance
    D.   Decreased efficiency and decreased maintenance

(A and B are correct/ A and D are correct/ A is correct/ B is correct)

B is correct

34. Do you heard about Wind Farm Simulation Software?

35. What is the specialty of Commonwealth Bay in Antarctica?
Windiest country of the world

CHAPTER 9

SOLAR ENERGY

1. What is the surface temperature of Sun?

    $(560^0C/260^0C/2600^0C/5600^0C)$

    5600^0C

2. Match the different instrumentation in relevance with Solar PV.

2a.

S.No	A	C.No	B
1	Compass	a	Irradiance
2	Clinometer	b	Sun's path diagram
3	Solar Path Finder	c	Solar irradiance
4	Pyranometer	d	Direction
5	Irradiance meter	e	Inclinometer

Ans: 1-d, 2-e, 3-b, 4-c, 5-a

2b.

S.No	A	C.No	B
1	Infrared	a	Voltage
2	Spirit	b	Wind
3	Vane	c	Sonic
4	Anemometer	d	Thermometer
5	Multimeter	e	Level

Ans: 1-d, 2-e, 3-b, 4-c, 5-a

3. In a classroom, student raised a question, why Indian solar panels are south faced? Professor replied with two following two statements.

   A. India lies in the northern hemisphere

   B. Panels faces equator to receive more light intensity

   (Statement A and B are correct/Statement A and B are relevant and incorrect/Statement A and B are not the answers to the question raised)

   Statement A and B are correct

4. Size of an inverter can be represented in? (KVA/W/Nm/Both A and B)
   KVA

5. SI unit of illuminance is? (Lux/Pears/Siemens/Unit less)
   Lux

6. In Solar PV system, row spacing and sun angles may be adjusted with a rule of?
   A thumb rule of 3.5 times height for row spacing to avoid shading effects and trigonometrically analyzing the altitude angle with the given time

7. What are CIGS and CdTe? What kind are they?
   Cadmium telluride (CdTe)

   Copper indium gallium selenides (CIGS)

   They are Polycrystalline materials applied for Solar PV

8. What is DSSC? (Dual Sensitive Solar Cells/Dutch type Short Solar Cells/Dye-Sensitized Solar Cells)
   Dye-Sensitized Solar Cells

9. Largest solar power plant in the world (Bhadla Park,India/ Roscoe, Texas/ Shalimar, India/ Kashiwazaki-Kariwa, Japan)
    Bhadla Park,India

10. What is NISE? Where it is located?
    National Institute of Solar Energy – Gurugram, Haryana

11. Saatvik, Vikram, TATA, Adani, Goldi – the group represents
    Top 10 Solar Panel Manufacturers in India

12. Name a technology through which invasion of endangered birds can be controlled using Renewable Energy?
    Solar Powered Bird Scarer

13. What is the Revised Solar Constant value and Old value?
    Old value – 1.353 w/sq.mt

    Revised value – 1368 w/sq.mt

14. What is Reflectance?
    The ratio of radiation reflected by a surface to the radiation incident on it.

15. What radiations do Pyranometer measures?
    Total Radiation and Indirect Radiation

16. In recent budget on Agriculture, most focus is laid on which part of renewable energy?
    Solar energy

17. Societies/Organizations for Renewable Energy
    SESI – Solar Energy Society of India

    ISES – International Solar Energy Society

    IRENA – International Renewable Energy Agency

    WBA – World Bioenergy Association

BDAI – Biodiesel Association of India

Global Wind Energy Council

World Wind Energy Association

International Hydropower Association

World Council for Renewable Energy

International Renewable Energy Alliance

INFORSE – International Network on Sustainable Energy

ANERT – Agency for Non Conventional Energy and Rural Technology

NERD – Non Conventional Energy and Rural Development Society

IBA – Indian Biogas Association

18. Name Materials out of which solar cells can be made
    Silicon, Perovskite, Polycrystalline

19. What is ALT in Solar Water Pumping? (All Location Test/Anti-lost Timer/No relevance/Android Located Test – rig)
    No relevance

20. What is VFD in Solar Water Pumping? (Variable Fertilizer Dump/ Variable Frequency Drive/No relevance/Inventor)
    Variable Frequency Drive

21. What are the PV Performance Parameters? How many interchanges required for perfect match? (0/1/Nil/2)

S.No	A	B
1	Maximum power current	I_{mp}
2	Short-circuit current	V_{mp}
3	Maximum power voltage	I_{sc}
4	Open-circuit voltage	V_{oc}
5	Maximum power	P_{mp}

Ans: 1

22. Match the suitable categories of UV radiation?

S. No.	Radiation	M. No.	Wavelength	M. No.	Travel
1	UV-A	A	Shorter	a	Upto Ozone layer
2	UV-B	B	Longer	b	Middle layer of human skin
3	UV-C	C	Shorter	c	Outer layer of human skin

Ans: 1 – B – b, 2 – C – c, 3 – A – a

23. Severe effects on human beings are caused by which type of UV radiation?

UV-C

24. Match the following

S. No.	A	M. No.	B
1	Wellington	**a**	Windiest country
2	Yuma	**b**	India's sunshine point
3	Gujarat	**c**	World Windiest city
4	Commonwealth Bay	**d**	Country of Winds
5	Denmark	**e**	World sunshine point

Ans: 1 – c, 2 – e, 3 – b, 4 – a, 5 – d

25. The majority of all PV systems installed to date are flat plate systems with fixed orientation. (True/False)

    True

26. Food Engineer says, 'Agricultural products, during sun drying the crop can either be dried or rewetted because of the hygroscopic properties'. Civil engineer says that food engineer's statement is incorrect. Who is right in their statements?

    Food engineer

27. Best heat transfer can be achieved with a porous material as (absorber/cover/insulator/water).

    Absorber

28. A___________ efficiency is obtained at a higher temperature if the solar air heater is double covered (higher/lower/poor/half)

    Higher

29. Black fabric, black-painted aluminum, or steel are the most common ________ materials at the moment (absorber/cover/frame/emitter)

    absorber

30. Polyurethane foam plates are well suited for _________ purposes.
    (Packaging/ Insulation/ Conducting/ Frame making)
    Insulation

31. The smallest independent operational unit of PV systems is the
    (solar cell/battery/charge controller/none)
    solar cell

32. For stand-alone systems, an inverter is required if dc loads are to
    be operated. (True/False)
    False

33. Additional functions of charge controller include (deep discharge
    protection of batteries/ system status indicators/ system survey /
    all of the above)
    all of the above

34. Two most important effects that must be taken into account for
    solar PV systems are variations in (temperature and pressure/
    temperature and humidity/irradiance and temperature/
    Temperature only)
    Irradiance and temperature

35. A. Dirt accumulation or partial shading are the problems in
    solar PV system
    B. Shaded cell act as load that consume the power that is
    generated by the other illuminated cells.
    (A is correct and B is the one of the reason/B is correct and A is
    the reason for B/ A and   B are wrong/ B is wrong reason for
    A which is partially correct)

    A is correct and B is the one of the reason

36. Solar energy finds its application in agriculture. Some of them
    are weeding, spraying, water pumping, drones and milking.

Scientist M says that above statement is partially correct. Scientist N says it is entirely wrong. Scientist A says that above statement is not at all correct. But Scientist O explained both of them with actual nature of statement. (Scientist M is correct on his stand/ Scientist O did a mistake/ Scientist N is perfectly correct than others/ None of the above)

None of the above

37. The solar tunnel dryer can be operated with one PV module (True/False)

True

38. Companies on Solar pumping systems compete with companies of (hand pumps/ animal-driven pumps/ electric motor-driven pumps/all of the above).

All of the above

39. Match the following in relevant to drone application in solar industry

S.No	A	C.No	B
1	Solar drone	a	Thermal imaging
2	Overheating	b	Shading effects
3	Topographic surveys	c	Footage
4	Seasonal sun positioning	d	High-pressure jet
5	Transmission line inspections	e	Maximum sunlight

Ans: 1-d, 2-a, 3-e, 4-b, 5-c

40. Universal scale for radiation measurements adopted in 1956 was (International Pyrheliometric Scale/Sun scale/International Pyrometer/Indian Pyranometer)

International Pyrheliometric Scale

41. Ratio of Monthly average of daily radiation on a horizontal surface to the monthly average extraterrestrial radiation is called as (Daily average cleanness index/Monthly average vortex index/ Monthly average intensity/ Monthly average cleanness index)

    Monthly average cleanness index

42. Match the following in relevant to drone application in solar industry

S.No	A	C.No	B
1	Concentration ratio	A	Ratio of average energy flux on receiver to that on the aperture
2	Local flux concentration ratio	B	Ratio of aperture area to receiver area
3	Flux concentration ratio	C	Ratio of flux at any point of the receiver to that on the aperture
4	Orientation system	D	Opening through which solar radiation enters
5	Aperture	e	Continuous or near continuous adjustments to compensate changing sun's position

   A. 1-a, 2-c, 3-b, 4-e, 5-d   B. 1-a, 2-b, 3-c, 4-d, 5-e

   C. 1-b, 2-a, 3-c, 4-e, 5-d   D. 1-b, 2-c, 3-c, 4-d, 5-e

    Ans: 1-b, 2-c, 3-a, 4-e, 5-d

43. Non-imaging and imaging types belongs to (Solar PV/ Concentrators/Spray Drones/Tractors)

    Concentrators

44. What is expansion for ASHRAE?

    American Society of Heating, Refrigerating and Air-Conditioning Engineers (ASHRAE)

45. What is the purpose of ray trace methods?

    Ray trace methods are used to analyze the concentrating collectors

46. National Renewable Energy Laboratory (NREL) has predicted that wind and solar will contribute 54% of India's renewable energy (RE) generation by (2017/2027/2047/2057).

    2047

47. Slar distillation units- Glass cover may have a thickness of (0.5 mm/4 mm/15 mm/None)

    4 mm

48. Solar ponds may have a depth of (1 to 15 m/ 1 to 100 m/ 1 to 3 m/ 1 to 1.5 m)

    1 to 3 m

49. Numerical experiments that can give results similar to physical experiments in solar thermal performance is called as (Hydration/ Superannuation/Simulation/Stimulation)

    Simulation

50. Design a solar powered weeder for vegetable fields.

51. Propose a concept applicable for utilization of solar power for protected cultivation machinery (not to be taken out of protected structure often)

52. Agri-Voltaic System – Discuss.

53. Give outline for solar powered GPS guided unmanned agricultural machinery

54. Solar powered (Sprayer/ drone/ weeder/ all the above) can be used in agriculture.

    All the above

55. Advantages of Bifacial Solar Panels

56. Describe about Space-Based Solar Power

57. Quantum dot solar cells use semiconductor nanoparticles to absorb light more efficiently across a broader spectrum. (True/ False)

    True

58. Leading countries in the development and implementation of solar-wind hybrid systems – list out.

59. Solar paint technologies (use light-sensitive materials/ generate electricity/ reduce yield of paddy/ both a and b)

    both a and b

60. Generally no moving parts and no specific thermal stresses are involved in technology?

    (Wind/ Hydro power/ Solar water heater/ Solar PV)

    Solar PV

CHAPTER 10
BIOENERGY

1. How biomass can be classified in major groups?

   1. Virgin Biomass

   2. Waste Biomass

2. Thermogravemetric Analysis is the alternative method for?
   Proximate Analysis

3. What are the major classification of biomass energy conversion?

   1. Biochemical Conversion

   2. Thermochemical Conversion

   3. Extraction

4. Waste Cooking Oil can be utilized effectively after recycling as a?
   Biodiesel

5. Activated Charcoal is otherwise called (Activated Cc/Activated Carbon/Both/None)
   Activated Carbon

6. What is the difference between obligate anaerobes and facultative anaerobes?

   Obligate anaerobes – Needs absence of oxygen strictly

   Facultative anaerobes – Can sustain in both presence and absence of oxygen

7. Biohythane is a hydrogen-methane blend with hydrogen. In the production of Biohythane, the two sequential anaerobic stages are?
   Dark fermentation followed by anaerobic digestion

8. State an application of Biohythane. (Food sector/Automotive Sector/Medicine/All the above)

    Automotive Sector

9. Carbon Molecular Sieves are derived from product A. Product A is derived from product B by single or multiple steps. Product A will be black and Product B will be mostly starts greenish. What are the products A and B?

    Product A – Activated carbon

    Product B – Biomass

10. Mention an application of Carbon Molecular Sieves in Bioenergy

    Gas Scrubbing

11. What is FTS in Bioenergy? What are the products involved?

    Fischer-Tropsch Synthesis – gives Hydrocarbons from Producer gas

12. What is the Torrefaction temperature?

    200 – 300° Celsius

13. Limits of Tar content in a producer gas for direct combustion is specified and IC engine application is not specified. (True/False)

    False

14. Nickel can be used as a catalyst for reducing the tar content. Scholar A says statement cannot be accepted. Whether Scholar A has to correct his statement?

    Yes

15. What is meant by supercritical water?

    Water above its critical temperature and pressure is said to be in supercritical state or simply as SCW.

16. What is BDTC in relation with Agricultural Engineering?

    Biogas Development and Training Centre

17. Biogas combustion also releases carbon dioxide though it was categorized as Green energy. What is the difference between biogas and natural gas in green concept?
    Biogas is carbon neutral. Biomass absorbing carbon dioxide while they alive as plants and releases Carbon dioxide when they are on combustion, hence they are carbon neutral. Natural gas is carbon is carbon positive, as they are converting the available carbon sink from the earth structure to carbon dioxide on combustion.

18. Combustion of biomass is GHG neutral. (True/False)
    True

19. In cow dung total solids, what percentage of volatile matter may be present?
    Around 80%

20. What amount of Ammonical nitrogen will stop methanogenesis completely? If above 3gm/liter can decrease the gas production?
    5 mg/liter

21. From houses, walls, buildings, the biogas plant should be constructed at least spacing?
    2 meter

22. Comparing Dheenbandhu model and KVIC model, which may be costlier to construct?
    KVIC

23. Biodiesel is produced from yeast. (True/ False/ Used along with other microbes/ none of these)
    False

24. PKV Waste fired dryer and Shell fired Copra dryer are of?
    Biomass fueled type

25. Bio oil and bio diesel are same. True/False/ Hypothetical/Varies based on product?

    False

    (Bio oil is a product of thermochemical conversion whereas biodiesel is a product of Extraction)

26. If a 20 kg dry cow dung is mixed with water and applied for biogas production, the biogas obtained will be 0.8 m^3. (True/False)

    False

27. Which is a mostly used equipment/device used for anotubes the thermal behavior of biomass?

    Thermogravemetric analyser

28. Give the products of wet biomass on hydrothermal treatment.

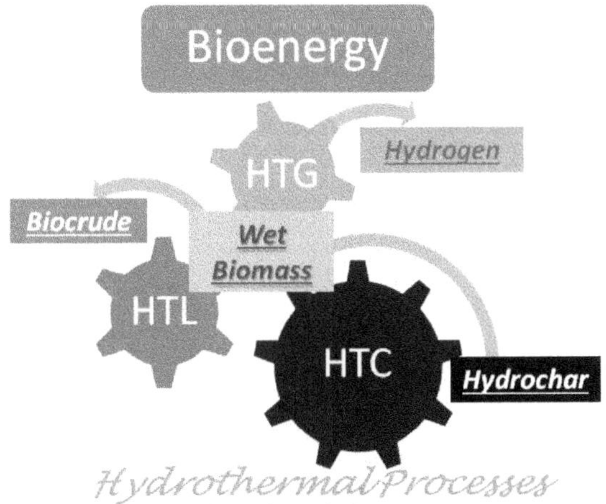

HTL – Hydrothermal Liquefaction, HTG – Hydrothermal Gasification, HTC – Hydrothermal Carbonization

Fig.1 Processing of Wet biomass through Hydrothermal Techniques to produce various state biofuels

29. What is the quantity of Hydrogen Sulphide present in the gobar gas?

    Traces

30. What is the optimum biogas to air ratio for complete combustion?

    One point six to seven

31. Dheenbandhu and Janata models of biogas plants were developed in the century of?

    *20*th

32. Name a difference between gram positive and gram negative bacteria.

    Gram negative bacteria have thin cell wall, whereas the gram positive bacteria have thick cell wall. Gram negative bacteria are more resistive as their cell wall is impenetrable.

33. What is the difference between obligate anaerobes and facultative anaerobes?

    Obligate anaerobe dies in the presence of Oxygen

    Facultative anaerobe shows better growth in presence of Oxygen but can also grow in absence of Oxygen also.

34. Name different models of Biogas plants.

    1. *KVIC (Khadi and Village Industries Commission) design.*

    2. *PRAD (Planning, Research and Action Division) design*

    3. *Murugappa Chettiar Research Centre design.*

    4. *Tamil Nadu Agricultural University dome type design*

    5. *ASTRA (Application of Science and Technology to Rural Areas) design*

    6. *Himachal Pradesh Capsule design*

    7. *Kacha-Pucca model of Punjab Agricultural University*

8. *Plug-flow design*

9. *AFPRO (Action for Food Production) design*

10. *Roorkee design*

11. *Deen Bhandhu design*

12. *Fibreglass fixed dome design (Underground model)*

13. *Mobile biogas plants*

14. *Plastic emulsion coated, heavily insulated, temperature controlled Switzerland biogas plants.*

15. *IARI (Indian Agricultural Research Institute) design*

16. *Ganesh Model*

17. *Ferro-cement Digester Biogas Plant*

35. Rice Husk and Rice straw, which gives lesser yields in biogasification?

Rice Straw

36. Ethanol has a smaller heat value but a higher octane rate than gasoline (True/False)

False

37. The problem of slurry water presence in gas outlet pipe is encountered mostly in which type of biogas plant? And give any reason for the problem.

Fixed dome. Problem may be due to higher slurry level in the digester

38. When a waste material is subjected to a composting process, its volume becomes increases. Whether the statement can be rejected?

Yes, statement can be rejected

39. A. Mesophilic temperature range – 25 to 45° Celsius

    B. Thermophilic temperature range - < 45° Celsius

    C. Biodegradation processes – least intense in the thermophilic phase

    Scholar A identified that C is incorrect, A and B are correct. But the Scholar B denied the   statement of Scholar A. Statement of Scholar A is (Correct/Incorrect)

    Correct

40. Match the following

S.No	Generation	C.No	Process
1	Fourth	a	FTS
2	Second	b	Algae cultivation
3	First	c	Biochemical Engineering
4	Third	d	Fermentation

    Ans: 1-c, 2-a, 3-d, 4-b

41. For determining thermal efficiency of a chulah, water boiling test is done (Yes/No)

    Yes

42. Single and double pot chulahs (TNAU/ CDB/ CIAE/ KAU)

    TNAU

43. Lignin decomposes at a temperature range of (280 to 500 F/ 280 to 380 deg C/ 280 to 380 F/ 280 to 500 deg C)

    280 to 500 deg C

44. Nithya said torrefaction is a endothermic process. Bharathi agrees with Nithya's statement. Whether it can be (Accepted/ Denied/ Modified/ Dinosaur)

    Accepted

45. Comparing pyrolysis, hydrothermal carbonization occurs at a
    _________ temperature
    Lower

46. In high pressure briquetting, binding agent is not needed, but
    additional binding materials are required for low pressure
    briquetting. Materials used as binding agent includes (Clay/
    Cow dung/ Both A and B/ Potato)
    Both A and B

47. Explain different types of briquetting

48. Find the odd one out (Switch grass/ Algae/ Camelina/ Tomato)
    Tomato

49. Find the odd one out (Soy beans/ Jatropha/ Maize/ Camelina)
    Maize

50. A. Real time monitoring of pH B. Predictive analytics for plant
    production optimization. C. Fire smoke alarms. All the three
    together were applications of
    (IoT in biogas systems/AI in Solar thermal plant/IoT in Wood
    stove/All the above)

    IoT in biogas systems

CHAPTER 11

NANOTECHNOLOGY

1. Nanomaterials have the potential to improve the economic viability of biodiesel production. (True/False)
   True

2. How Nanotechnology helps in Biogas Production improvement?
   Several types and kinds of Nanomaterial additives are used to increase the biogas production yield.

3. Name few nano additives
   Nano TiO, Nano CeO, Nano Zero Valence Iron (NZVI)

4. How Nanotechnology can be applied in Wind mill blades?
   Stronger and light weight blades can be made by the use of nanotubes-filled epoxy.

5. How thin films with Cu based nanodots helps Solar Panels?
   Increase efficiency, Reduce material needed and reduced price.

6. Solar PV recycling is going to be a challenge in the future. Mention any of the method to recycle the Solar cells.
   CNC – Cellulose nanocrystals

   Devices made on these substrates can be easily dissolved in water, allowing semiconducting materials and metal layers to be filtered and recycled.

7. Name a nanotechnology application in farm machinery
   Coating of cutting blades or knives

8. Harvesting blades coated with a nano material had a reduced specific shearing energy. (Correct/Incorrect)

   Correct

9. Name a nano material used for coating cutting blades in agriculture.

   TiO_2 (Titanium dioxide) nanoparticles within the Ni (Nickel) matrix

10. Nano Urea Liquid was launched by?

    IFFCO (Indian Farmers Fertilizer Cooperative Limited)

11. Nanocoatings not improve the scratch and abrasion resistance. (True/False)

    False

12. Father of Indian Nanotechnology.

    Prof. C.N.R Rao

13. A. Use of nanocomposites in manufacturing can reduce the weight of the component.

    B. Nanospray extends the shelf life of the fruit.

    (Both the statements A and B are useful to farm machinery/ Statement A is useful to farm machinery/ Statement B is alone suiting farm machinery/ None of the statements related to farm machinery)

    Statement A is useful to farm machinery

14. Slow release technology is associated with (Fertilizer management/Food chain/Farm Tillage/None)

    Fertilizer management

15. Carbon nanotubes assists in retention of seed moisture (True/ False)

    True

16. Nano refinement of tannery effluent is not possible(True/False)

    False

17. Scientist A stated that nano barcode applicability in seed encoding. Scientist B stated about 'Au' and its usefulness in seed protection. Scientist C refused to accept Scientist A and B, and stated about the Lithium chloride involvement in a colour change from blue to pink. Now find out the scientists who were correct with their statements. (A only/A and B/A and C/All three)

    All three

18. Expand AFM

    Atomic Force Electron Microscope (AFM)

19. Rearrange the following pairs. Fuel additives- Lighter in weight, Structural chassis – Tires, Engine blocks – Emissions, CNT – Lighter in weight

    Fuel additives – Emissions, Structural chassis – Lighter in weight, Engine blocks – high temperatures, CNT – Tires

20. Nanotechnology is subjected to following issues. A. Legal, B.Policy, C.Ethical. Find out the possible issue (A and B are suitable/All are suitable/None/C only).

    All are suitable

21. Sort out the group with suitable terms possible with nano technology (Slow, Quick, pH release/ Heat, Moisture, pH release/ Slow, pH, Moisture release/ All the above)

    All the above

22. Match the following

S. No.	A	M. No.	B
1	Hydrophilic	a	Hydrophobic
2	Alkanes	b	Water hating
3	Hydrophobic	c	Water loving

Ans: 1 – c, 2 – a, 3 – b

23. In drones, Nano category refers to size (less than 200 grams/ Upto 249 grams/more than 10 mm/equal to less than 250 grams)

Upto 249 grams

24. Nano-sized semiconductor particles known as quantum dots (True/False)

True

25. Find the odd one out (Blade coating/ Phosphorus/Solar cells/ SPAD meter) from nanotechnology point of view.

SPAD meter

CHAPTER 12

PRECISION AGRICULTURAL MACHINERY

1. For precision spraying applications, it can take help from either GIS or GPS?

   Both

2. What is HTML full form?

   Hyper Text Markup Language

3. What is the shortform referred for Hyper Text Transfer protocol?

   HTTP

4. What is the expansion of QR in QR Code?

   Quick Response Code

5. *The term which* refers to the control of unknown plants with unknown dynamics subject to unknown disturbances is called as?

   Robust control

6. TCS – (Traction Control System/ Tata Consultancy Services/ Both are correct)

   Both are correct

7. Give an example of deterministic model

   Model for Conversion of Degree Celsius to Fahrenheit

8. What are DEM and FEM?

    Discrete Element Method

    Finite Element Method

9. Name some DEM softwares.

    Edem, Rocky dem

10. What is ICTs?

    Information and Communication Technology

11. Name some software for Statistics and/or Statistical Analysis

    "R" and "SPSS"

12. Name any Application of ArcGIS Software in Farm Machinery

    Variable Rate Fertilizer Application, Mapping processes

13. What is Information in the Data point of view?

    Processed Data is called Information

14. List the terms in Data Science

    Data acquisition, Data warehousing, Data guardians, Data management, Data mining, Data refinement, Data Processing, Data randling, Data exploration, Data cleaning or preparation

15. What is BIGDATA? State an example

    Data that is huge in size, which may grow exponentially with time. It is an Unstructured and Unsupervised Data, Example: Results returned on Google Search by searching any Title.

16. What are the types of Big Data?

    Structured

    Unstructured

    Semi-structured

17. Name some big data tools

    Apache Hadoop, Apache Spark, Apache Storm

18. Find the odd one out (Ansys Fluent/ Dassault Systèmes/ Unigraphics/OriginLab)

    OriginLab

19. {GPS, GLONASS, BeiDou, EGNOS, SBAS}- From this set,

    a. One is odd

    b. Two were odd

    c. No odd items

    d. Non-related items

    c. No odd items

20. LCC stands for (Leaf Coding Colour/Leaf Chart Colour/Leaf Colour Chart/Life Changing Candle)

    Leaf Colour Chart

21. Wi-Fi, Bluetooth, Zigbee, Cellular networks are under the term (Connectivity/Data collection/Data Communication/Data Processing)

    Connectivity

22. Match the following

S.No	A	M.No	B
1	Narrow AI	**a**	Facts
2	F1 Score	**b**	Weak AI
3	Surpass human intelligence	**c**	Harmonic mean of precision and recall
4	Rule based system	**d**	Performance
5	Confusion Matrix	**e**	Super AI

Ans: 1-b, 2-c, 3-e, 4-a, 5-d

23. Nitrogen Use Efficiency (NUE)

    a. High NUE: Indicates efficient use of nitrogen

    b. By calculating NUE, farmers and agronomists cannot estimate the effectiveness of nitrogen management practices

    c. Pollution is not associated with this term.

    d. It is a ratio of Output of Nitrogen in Plant Product to the input nitrogen

    (a,b,c,d are correct/a, b, c are correct/ a and b are correct, c and d are incorrect/ c and d are correct/ None of the above)

    None of the above

24. Why it is important for a Farm Machinery Engineer to know about NUE?

    By focusing on improving Nitrogen Use Efficiency (NUE), engineers can contribute to more sustainable, profitable, and efficient agricultural practices through research and development on machinery, innovative designs of fertilizer application equipment, optimization, and precise fertilizer metering.

25. Hyperspectral data sets typically have (100–200/2-3/5-6/1 lakh)

    100–200

26. Full form of SPAD in SPAD meter (Soil Plant Analysis Device/ Soon Pilot Angry Device/Static Plant Activity Denoter/Soil Plant Analysis Development)

    Soil Plant Analysis Development

27. What is VRT?

    Variable Rate Technology

28. What is proximity sensor?

    A proximity sensor is a sensor able to detect the presence of nearby objects without any physical contact.

29. Two types of Varied Rate Technology include Map-based control and Real-time control (True/False)

    True

30. What is KML file?

    Keyhole Markup Language

31. One important use of time-based GIS technology involves creating time-lapse photography that shows processes occurring over large areas and long periods of time.

    (Statement is correct/ Statements is wrong/ Statement is irrelevant/ None of the above)

32. Major Components of GIS includes

    (Hardware/Software/Data/All the above)

    All the above

33. Most relevant hardware support for GIS applications includes

    (Scanner/Digitizer/pH meter/Both A & B)

    Both A & B

34. A. The performance of GNSS is not assessed using 4 criteria namely, Accuracy, Integrity, Continuity, and Availability

    B.   GPS is the most prevalent GNSS

    (Both the statements are correct/ Both the statements are wrong/ One is correct and other is wrong/ None of the above)

    One is correct and other is wrong

35. The difference between receivers' measured and real position, speed or time is referred as

    Accuracy

36. PNT refers to Positioning, Navigation and?
(Tuning/Teaching/Training/Timing)

Timing

37. 100 cm accuracy means the represented location of a feature may be how far from its true location.
(As far as 1000 cm/As near as 100 cm/exactly 1000 cm/ As far as 1000 mm)

As far as 1000 mm

38. Yield monitoring system uses various sensors. One among them was travel speed sensor (True/False)

True

39. Which of the following is a tool for precision agriculture?
(GPS only/GPS and GIS/Cow/Both B and C)

GPS and GIS

40. Match the following

S. No.	A	M. No.	B
1	Ranging error	a	Pixel
2	Raster data	b	Distance
3	Vector data	c	Known values
4	Control Points	d	Point

Ans: 1 – b, 2 – a, 3 – d, 4 – c

41. Match the following

S. No.	A	M. No.	B
1	Remote Sensing	a	Ground based Robots
2	Chlorophyll	b	Vehicle mounted Green Seeker
3	Proximal sensing	c	Unmanned Aerial Vehicle
4	NDVI	d	SPAD

Ans: 1 – c, 2 – d, 3 – a, 4 – b

42. What is the difference between DEM and DSM?

    DSM (Digital Surface Model): Represents the Earth's surface including all natural and man-made features like buildings and trees.

DEM (Digital Elevation Model): Shows the elevation of the Earth's surface, excluding buildings and trees, focusing solely on terrain height.

43. a. Expand YOLO

    b. Machine learning is simple comparing Deep learning

    c. Deep learning is suitable for structured data only.

    Answers for the a, b, and c are (order not followed)

    (You Only Look Once, False, True, / Young Object Looking Orchestra/ Youth Organization on Land Ownership, True, False/ Youth Only Look Once, True, False,)

    You Only Look Once, True, False

44. {Pix4D Mapper, Agi Soft, NDVI, NDRE, Georeferencing} – Most relevant word to this set is (Precision nutrition/Precision mapping/Ploughing/Pest identification)

    Precision mapping

45. Match the following

S.No	A	M.No	B
1	Latency	a	Subset of Artificial intelligence
2	CNN	b	Architecture
3	Machine learning	c	Evaluation
4	Precision	d	Network
5	True positive	e	Predicts correct

Ans: 1-d, 2-b, 3-a, 4-c, 5-e

46. Match the following

S.No	A	M.No	B
1	False Negative	a	China
2	Apple	b	Performance
3	Trimble	c	Herbicide production
4	ESP	d	Tech. company
5	Bayer	e	Microcontroller

Ans: 1-b, 2-c, 3-e, 4-a, 5-d

47. Telematics applies to remote monitoring of equipments (True/ False)

True

48. Select the term from column A having most possible number of matches from column B.

S.No	A	M.No	B
1	Google Earth Pro	a	Open source
2	Agi Soft	b	NDVI
3	Pix4D	c	Delineation
4	Quantum GIS	d	Mapping
5	DJI GS Pro	e	IDW

4. Quantum GIS

49. What is kriging?

50. Differentiate between raster and vector data.

51. If you are allotted with a task of site-specific pesticide application, what method you prefer out of prescription map based and real-time (on the go)? And why? Answer from your point of view.

52. Accuracy of GPS may be affected by Atmospheric Effects, Physical Obstructions, Numerical Miscalculations. The above statement was given by a masters' scholar A. On the other hand masters' scholar B says that there was a irrelevant factor listed in the statement. Now, doctoral scholar A has to give the confirmation on their conversation. What should be the doctoral scholar A's reply on masters' scholar A? (Its correct/Not correct/ Partially correct/Masters scholar B is correct)

Its correct

53. Soil sampling for variable rate application is also same like soil sampling to determine the field average for a single rate application. (True/False)

False

   A. The common approach to achieve systematic soil sampling is to overlay a rectangular grid on a map or photograph of the field

   B. The common approach to achieve systematic soil sampling is to overlay a square grid on a map or photograph of the field

   C. Any one of the statement (A or B) was correct and the other was wrong

54. Identify the correct statements (A & B/ A & C/ B & C/All three A, B, C)

A & B

55. Expand NMEA (Natural Management of Entomological Affects/ National Marine Electronics Association/ National Machinery and Equipment Association of America/ National Machinery and Equipment Association)

    National Marine Electronics Association

56. The baud rate is a measure of the speed at which data is transmitted over a communication channel (Yes/No)

    Yes

57. What are the 10 Vs' of big data?

58. Volatility of data and Velocity of data are exactly the same (May be/ May not be/ Both are irrelevant terms/ Not the same)

    Not the same

59. Give a concept of a precision agriculture machine, other than precision seeder, fertilizer applicator or pesticide spraying.

60. List out some field mapping tools

61. Find the odd one out (ArcGIS/ Pix4D mapper/ AgriVijay/ AgiSoft)

    AgriVijay

62. Find the odd one out (GreenSeeker/ SPAD/ Yara-N sensor/ Garmin unit)

    Garmin unit

63. Name a open firmware for training a machine vision model.

64. Describe about existing or give an idea for

    a. Crop weed signalling techniques

    b. Image processing based inter and intra row weeder

    c. Robotic spraying arm

CHAPTER 13
DRONES

1. What is the classification of drones based on weight and licensing?

    Nano drone (<0.25 kg) (Upto 15 m)

    Micro drone (0.25 to 2 kg) (Upto 60 m)

    Small drones (2 to 25 kg)

    Medium drones (25 to 150 kg)

    Large drones (>150 kg)

2. Name few physical types of drones.

    Multi-rotor, Fixed-wing, Single-rotor helicopter, Fixed-Wing Hybrid Drones

3. Excluding those in the Nano category, state some mandatory requirements for drones flown in Indian sub continent.

    GPS

    Return to Home

    Anti collision light

    ID plate

    NPNT (No Permission, No take off)

4. What is Digital Sky platform?

    An online platform hosted by the Directorate General of Civil Aviation (DGCA) for various activities related to the management of unmanned aircraft system activities in India.

All drone operators will register their drone and request permission to fly for each flight through India's Digital Sky Platform.

5. "Fly in VLOS". What does it mean in terms of drone?

   VLOS – visual line of sight, "Fly in VLOS" means be within visual range of drone.

6. Find out the odd terms out.

   (UAV – Drones – Aircraft without pilot/passenger – Precision spraying – Deep subsoiling – Remote sensing – motor power difference)

   Deep subsoiling

7. Match the following

S. No.	A	M. No.	B
1	Home lock and Course lock	a	Identification
2	UAOP	b	Regulatory body in civil aviations
3	UIN	c	License
4	DGCA	d	Drone
5	Digital sky	e	Online platform

Ans: 1 – d, 2 – b, 3 – a, 4 – c, 5 – e

8. A drone have meaning as?

   (Unmanned aerial vehicle/ Male honey bee/ Sound/ All the above)

   All the above

9. Front right propeller of the drone will be always [Black & brown = 10 Clock wise = 5 Counter clock wise = 2   Anti-clock   wise = 3 Non-rotating = 4 Fixed in 2 cm more height = 6 Operated

by BLDC motors = 7]. Select relevant answer and what may be the summed value of the equivalent numbers to relevant answer. (10/15/12/11)

12

10. Cause – icing, what are the effects? (ice build up in leading edge/ gimbal locking/ pilot discomfort/all the above)

All the above

11. Any accident should be reported to DGCA within

12. Minimum education qualification in India for drone pilot certification - _S_C _ _S_ - Find the missing letter with or without repetition – (S, L, A, P/ A, D, Q, M/ S, P A, W/ R, P, T, O)

S, L, A, P

13. What is the importance of a type certificate for drones?

14. Some of the numbers are given here along with matching alphabetic letter. [5 – A, 3 – B, 4 – C]

    Find a suitable pairs of A and C (Red and Green/Green and Red/ Outer Yellow and Red/ Red and Outer Yellow) and what does the numbers with A, B and C may represent? (Radius/ Distance/ Height/ None).

Option	Question 1	Question 2
Brass	Red and Outer Yellow	Distance
Silver	Red and Green	Radius
Iron	Red and Outer Yellow	Radius
Gold	Outer Yellow and Red	None

Iron

15. Rank the following columns

A	B	C	D	E	F	G
Signal loss	Trainer	Battery	RGB	2-3	3-2	3-1
Electronic speed controller	Autonomous	4	Green	4-2	2-4	4-2
C Rating	Sensor	RTH	RPTO	3-1	4-1	1-3
Quadcopter	G	Speed	Mapping	1-4	1-3	2-4

Match any two columns of A, B, C and D to form a pair. Guess the correct two different pairs and match number column (E, F, G) must provide matching for both the pairs

(E/F/G/H)

G

16. Brain of the drone is usually refers to?

    Flight controller

17. A drone category which can operate without insurance? (VTOL/ Agri/Nano/Nano & micro)

    Nano

18. What is a C2 link and heart of drone?

19. For effective flying of a drone, transmitter requires how many channels? (1/22/4/5)

    4

20. Red zone is otherwise called as (Dark orange zone/No-fly zone/ Sad zone/Prohibited square)

    No-fly zone

21. What is RPAS?

    Remote Pilot Aviation System

22. Maximum altitude limit in inner yellow zone is (200 m/200 dm/200 ft/400 ft/400 m)

    200 ft

23. Name the component provided in drone to prevent shaking effect in camera. (Gimbal/Dumbell/Shutter/Electronic Spring)

    Gimbal

24. Which will have more endurance? Scholar A said it was fixed wing aircrafts. Professor denied scholar A statement since he don't have enough awareness on this subject. Whether scholar A is correct on his statement? (Yes/No)

    Yes

25. Airspace is unavailable on digisky (True/False)

    False

26. Find the missing word and matching word for the whole phrase

    Dynamic Remotely _____________ Navigation Equipment

    (Controlled & Tractor attachment/ Controlled & UAV/ Operated & UAS/ Guided & GPS)

    Operated & UAS

27. A drone was owned by a business man and the weight of the drone was 24.5 kg. In his business firm, he was the first only person acquired a remote pilot certificate of small category. His business was expanded to agriculture sector and there was a need to utilize the drone for his business in agriculture. So, near Goa, his manager started operating the drone. But there was criticism rose that the action was over-rule. What may be the over-rule? *Business man owns a remote pilot license but not his manager.*

28. A hexacopter is having _________ BLDC motors

    A W XYZ PTO shaft comprises _________ splines

    Hint: W = 10000-9360, X = Next letter of Q, Y = Previous letter of Q, Z = First letter of the word machine.

    (6/34/12/11)

    6

29. A. Full form of RPTO was Remote Pilot Training Organization.

    B. Full form of ROPS was Roll Over Protection System.

    C. Full form of RPM was

    (Roll Protection Mode/ Revolution Begin Moment/Revolutions Per Minute/ Both A & C)

    Revolutions Per Minute

30. Mechanism for turning the face direction of wind-mill and drone was referred as (Roll/Pitch/Yaw/Throttle)

    Yaw

31. Name a two different type of shots performed by multispectral imaging drone.

    Timed interval shot and distance interval shot

32. There were two pilots (A&B) having each one drone with same level of battery voltage. Pilot A flying the drone by moving forward and rearward. Pilot B was taking off and landing the drone continuously. Now, a single soft drink bottle was waiting for the pilot who comes first after exhausting battery in their drones. Pilot A had the soft drink and later pilot B came by exhausting the battery. What is the probability of any of the pilot had cheated?

33. A. The Component controlling the speed of BLDC motors in drone is referred here as Y.

    B. Top-left key in a laptop keyboard written shortly as X.

    C. What is the chance of X and Y are same?

34. Drone spray characteristics can be evaluated by?
    (Anemometer, tachometer, vernier caliper, digital camera/water sensitive paper/dynamometer/All the above)

    Water sensitive paper

35. Charging the battery>Preflight checks>DEFGH>Spraying> Landing
    (Arming/ Filling & Take-off/Both A and B in same order/Both A and B in different order)

    Both A and B in different order

36. What is the opinion on the statement drone spraying reducing health hazards comparing knapsack sprayer?

37. The options Brake, Avoid and Off are related to a sensor (GPS/ Temperature/Proximity/Nil)
    Proximity

38. A. NPNT is implemented. B. NPNT is not followed C. NPNT is No picnic No tour D. With regard to aviations NPNT is unusual term.
    Which are/is the positive statement? (A and C/ A and B/ A and D/ A only, not C)

    A only, Not C

39. No drone zone – Beyond F distance (horizontal & unit is referred as G) into sea from the coastal line, if the ground station for drone control is at stable land platform. From the following

options, which may yield F value when G is in meters? (0+0/ 0+50/ 50+50+1/ 251+249)

251+249

40. VloS – Visual _______ of Sight

Seed drill is meant for _______Sowing

Find the missing word in both sentences (Legumes/Lead/ Light(ly)/Line)

Line

41. A.   Every drone must have a Unique Identification _____________

B.   540 is a _________

C.   Sales of a sprayer can be represented as ___________

With respect to A and B answer, what answer may C may have? (Number/ Percentage/ Alphanumeric/ None)

Number

42. Aspee, Sprayer, K++, Flight controller, DJI, Drone, Tattu, ABC – ABC is (Drone/ Sticker/ Art/ Battery)

Battery

43. What is loiter mode?

44. Double the number of X is Y. Y is the radius of Red zone (for drones). Z is half of Y. Z is 10 km. (True/False).

False

45. A.   Flying a drone

B.   Riding a tractor

C.   Operating a robotic harvester

D.   Running a autonomous grading machine

Rank according to skill requirement (higher the first, lower the last)

46. A.   50% subsidy for drones

    B.   Lowering the price of drones

    C.   Free Remote pilot certification training for marginal scale farmers

    D.   Free drones for large farmers with certification

    E.   Agricultural Engineering Department offered custom hiring of drones exclusively for marginal and small farmers.

    Rank the importance according to your policy.

47. A.   Flying drone without a remote pilot certificate

    B.   Using a drone to threaten birds

    C.   Spraying a over dosed herbicide on a food crop cultivation with drone

    D.   Using a drone without co- pilot

    E.   Flying a medium class drone in a residential area during night time without light.

    Rank the harmfulness & risk involved in these cases.

48. Bala was a pilot holding a medium category Remote pilot certificate, so that he can fly upto 150 kg weighing drone. He was flying a 24.5 kg drone and met with and unfortunate accident. He reported the accident to the authority after 71 hours. No question was on correct number required. What was not correct in this case? (150/24.5/71/48)

    71

49. While flying a drone with obstacle avoidance sensor at its front, scholar Murugan was pitch forwarding. A tree was at front of its path. What may happen, if Murugan has not identifies the tree?

50. Rank the following columns

A	B	C	D	E	F
Milk	Hand-doing	Large	I	I	IV
Germination	Automated	Nano	IV	III	I
Tillering	Powered	Small	III	IV	II
Panicle initiation	Mechanical	Medium	II	II	III

Select the most relevant column for ranking or sequential order matching 3 different columns A, B, and C. (D/E/F/None)

F

51. A Drone is at G location. In front of G, there was a 20 m high post. Backside of G there was a clear space. Left side of a G, there was a tree. Right side of a G, Athira was standing and operating the drone. The drone has obstacle avoidance sensor at rear side. Can Athira pitch rearward for 3 Meter followed by pitch forward for 2.5 meter? (Yes/no)

Yes

52. A Drone is at J location. In front of J, there was a 10 m high post. Backside of J there was no clear space. Left side of a J, there was a tree. Right side of a J, Vetri was standing and operating the drone. The drone has obstacle avoidance sensor at rear side. Can Vetri pitch rearward for 5 Meter followed by pitch forward for 3.5 meter? (Yes/no)

No

53. What are the major drawbacks of drone technology in agriculture?

54. Drones are booming all around the world in various sectors. What is your point of view in drone application for agricultural input delivery systems?

55. What are the rules and regulations in India needs for improving and sustaining the drone technology in the nation?

56. Enumerate any 5 different farm applications of drone other than spraying.

57. Think and say the practical adoption of drone based fertilizer applicator – Drone bird scarer – Drone harvester for coconut.

58. Name the applications (agri/non-agri) of way-point based autonomous flight option.

59. Give a innovative idea (completely unexplored till now) for research in drones

60. Select a good combination of imaging parameters (height of fly, horizontal & lateral overlap %) for a multispectral mapping (120 m, 75% / 30 m, 75% / 5 m, NIL/ 60 m, 20%).
    30 m, 75% overlap

CHAPTER 14
MECHATRONICS AND ROBOTICS

1. Absolute encoder provides a unique position value (True/ False)
   True

   (A) HMI is the Human Machine Interface. (B) HMI dashboard or screen used to control   machinery. (C) Statement A and B are wrong.

2. What is the nature of statement C? (True/ False)
   False

3. What is the mechanism involved in servo?
   Negative feedback mechanism

4. What is MEMS?
   Micro-Electro-Mechanical Systems – miniaturized mechanical and electro- mechanical elements (i.e., devices and structures) that are made using the techniques of microfabrication.

5. What is the difference between simulation and odelling?

6. Arduino and Raspberry Pi
   Both have the same functions, but have slight variations and differences in application areas. Raspberry Pi is a mini computer, with Linux operating System.

   Arduino is a microcontroller mother board. Arduino may have single operation whereas Raspberry Pi shall have multiple operations.

7. What is PLC? (Programmable Logic Controller, a type of computer/ Printed Light Controller, a type of computer/ Pinned Logic Controller, a type of robot/ Positive Logic Comparer, a type of robot)

   Programmable Logic Controller, a type of computer

8. What is the speciality about Taiwan with reference to Semiconductor Manufacturing Companies?

   Globally, Taiwan has the largest chip manufacturing hub

9. (A) Servo is a motor under control engineering (B) Servomechanism is shortened as servo. Say the true or false in both the statements

   (Both are correct/ Both are wrong/ A is correct, B is wrong/ B is correct, A is wrong)

   Both are correct

10. Stepper motors are (DC motors/ Stepping motors/ Brushless electric motor/ All are suitable answers)

    All are suitable answers

11. Elaborate application of Raspberry Pi in Farm Machinery

12. What is the industrial name for 3D printing? (Three doctoral printing/Three dimensional view/ALM – Additive Layer Manufacturing/Discounted precise builder)

    ALM (Additive Layer Manufacturing)

13. What is meant by DGPS?

    Differential Global Positioning System

14. DGPS involves how much number of receivers?

    2

15. Match the following with respect to drones

S. No.	A	M. No.	B
1	ESC	a	Electronic Speed Controller
2	UAOP	b	Top right key in computer
3	DoF	c	Unmanned Aircraft Operator Permit
4	DGCA	d	Power Distribution Board
5	PDB	e	Post Doctoral Byelaws
		f	Directorate General of Civil Aviation (India)
		g	Division of General Civil Aviations (New Delhi)
		h	Department of Finance
		i	Degrees of Freedom

Ans: 1 – a, 2 – c, 3 – i, 4 – f, 5 – d

16. Relationship between Python and Java?

Python is a simplified form of Java

17. Describe some facts about Arduino.

Simply stating, Arduino is the brain for a Robot or an integrated environment. Arduino is a set of Microcontroller (a physical circuit board) and Software (Integrated Development Environment) runs on a Computer, where the coding has to be uploaded to operate the microcontroller. The Arduino can interact with motors, GPS units, Cameras, Internet and Machines. Language applied for coding may be C++.

18. What is P&P which is related to robotics?

Pick and Place

19. Joseph F. Engelberger (Father of mechatronics/American President/Tamil Poet/Father of Robotics)

Father of Robotics

20. A standardized programming language used to control Computer Numerical Control (CNC) machines such as robotic arms (S code/C code/G code/None)

    G code

21. Match the B and D column and check corresponding A and C column. Count the number of original colour in A column matching with fruit in C column.

A	B	C	D
Red	EDEM	Banana	Lathe
Green	3D printer	Apple	Urea flow in hopper
Blue	CNC	Orange	Welding

    Ans: 3 (Red apple, Green grapes, Orange orange)

22. Match the following

A	B	C	D
1	Mecanum wheels	a)	Python
2	Image processing	b)	Mega and Nano
3	Ardunio	c)	Climbing robot
4	Jupyter	d)	MatLab

    Ans:1-c, 2-d, 3-b, 4-a

23. Programming robot – Teaching method, Actuators – Motion, Servo motor – feedback, Linear motor actuator – Positioning, Rotary encoder – Bulb, Gantry – non-linear robot

    How many pairs are not matching correctly? (4/6/0/2)

    2

24. Scara robot is created by Japanese – (True/False)

    True

25. End effectors motions (Rotating motion/Up & down motion/ Holding/All the above)

    All the above

26. A. Revolute joints powered by a servo motor

    B. Prismatic joints powered by a pneumatic system or hydraulic unit

    C. Spherical joints have two degrees of freedom only

    (A, B and C are correct/All are correct/A and C are correct/C is incorrect)

    C is incorrect

27. Address important disadvantages of servo motor and stepper motor.

28. Suggest a new robotic design concept for sugarcane crop mechanization.

29. How degrees of freedom can be calculated?

30. Constraints are not necessary at all (Yes/No)

    No

31. Which type of sensor is commonly used to measure soil moisture levels?

    (Optical sensor/ Capacitive sensor/ Temperature sensor/ Ultrasonic sensor)

    Capacitive sensor

32. One of the purposes of using sensors in agricultural mechatronics is to (control the weather/ monitor environmental conditions/ increase fuel consumption/reduce crop yield)

    Monitor environmental conditions

33. A. The term mechatronics was introduced by Yasakawa Electric

    B. The term mechatronics was introduced in 1969

    (Statement A and B are true and not relevant/ Statement A and B are false but relevant/ Statement A and B are true and relevant/ I don't know the answer)

    Statement A and B are true and relevant

34. Give the differences between

    1. Feedback and signal

    2. Sensors and actuators

    3. Micro controllers and microprocessors

    4. DMA and IRQ data transfers

    5. Precision and accuracy

35. Nyquist Frequency – Explain

36. A. Actuator motion

    B. Band pass filter

    (A is a robotic action and B is a processing equipment/ A is a source and B is a remedy/ A is a old technology and B is latest/ A is source of noise and B is enhancer of noise)

    A is a source and B is a remedy

37. Rejects frequencies in the range and allow others to pass – This is represents a type of (Noise/Signal/Filter/Amplifier)

    Filter

38. Identify the component with the following features

    A. No rotor heat dissipation problems

    B. Does not require maintenance to replace worn brushes

    C. Create less EMI

(DC stator/A and B represents BLDC motors but C doesnot/ BLDC motors/ Each statement represents different components)

BLDC motors

39. Scholar A wrote a sentence in an exam conducted by National body as 'difference between AC and DC motors is in the inherit ability to control speed'. But the evaluator A considered this as wrong. When applied for re-evaluation, evaluator B also considered it to be wrong. If you are given a chance of evaluating this question, what will you decide?

    A. Wrong because the other two evaluators considered as wrong

    B. Right, since it was third evaluation

    C. Decision upon referring to original statement/fact

    D. Scolding evaluators A and B

    Decision upon referring to original statement/fact

40. A. The bus is a central nervous system of the computer.
    B. Flight controller is the brain of the drone
    C. Farm machinery is a sub-discipline of Agri Engineering

    (B and C are correct, A is wrong/ All are wrong/ B is correct C is entirely wrong/ A is correct)

    A is correct

41. C-space – What does it imply on robotics?

42. Match the following

S.No	A	M.No	B
1	Full joints	a)	Lower pair
2	Half joints	b)	Relates
3	Joins	c)	Higher pair

Ans: 1-a, 2-c, 3-b

43. Global population is expected to be X million by 2050 according to Y

A	XXXX	B	YYYY
Red	9600	Lemon	IRRI
Green	96	Beans	US
Yellow	960	Tomato	FAO

With suitable X and Y answers, corresponding A and B match practically? (Yes/No)

Yes

44. Think like humans and mimic their action (AI/ Farm robot/ Big data/ Monolaurine)

AI

45. Duck was a robot invented for the purpose of (Running/ Transplanting/ Insect capture/ Weeding)

Weeding

46. When we can expect 6G adoption in India?

47. Explain the performance parameters of precision planter which works based on mechatronics.

48. What do you understand by the term humanoid?

49. Identify and infer about the world's leading drone manufacturing country.

50. Do you which is the world's smallest humanoid robot?

51. What is the role of biomimetics in agricultural robotic design?

52. Can you name two mechatronic applications of mechatronics in Indian agriculture with wider adoption?

53. Based on the sensing, what are the different types of encoders available?

54. ROS is an (Robot/Operating system/ Integrating system/ Computer component/ Mimicry audio)

    Operating system

55. What are the common challenges in present horticultural farming to adopt robots in your perspective?

56. Select the perfect group of possible agricultural applications of robotic arms

    A. Transplanting, Packaging & spraying

    B. Ploughing, Wood carving, drone spraying

    C. Autonomous tractor, Giant wheel, sprinkler

    (A and B/ B and C/ A and C/ A only)

    A only

57. Select any one cash crop. What will be the most prioritized option for robotic research in the selected crop?

58. With respect to robotics and automation, AI and BD commonly may be (Awareness index and Bulk density/ Artificial intelligence and Bagged Data/ Artificial intelligence and Big data/ Allowable limits and Board of Deep learning)

    Artificial Intelligence and Big Data

59. In combine harvesters, what are the possible applications of robotics?

60. Design a robotic system for autonomous spraying of pesticides in a vine yard.

61. Manjunath's team is in the process of designing a robot intended for use in a vineyard. Given that the land is leveled but the grapevines are at varying heights, the robot requires a flexible platform that can be raised and lowered as needed. As a member

of Manjunath's team, how would you propose to design the mechanism for this adjustable platform?

62. Explain the working of automatic milking machine.

63. Arasu's team is developing a robotic harvester for an apple orchard. Considering that the apple trees vary in height and the terrain is uneven, the robot needs a stable, adjustable platform that can navigate the slopes and reach apples at different heights. As a member of Arasu's team, how would you approach designing this adaptable platform?

64. Saiprasanth is working on a robotic capsicum harvesting machine. He was having a trouble with developing a detection system for identifying the matured green capsicum. Help him with some ideas for identifying the maturity of green capsicum. Note that, he already developed machine vision based detection system for yellow capsicum maturity identification.

65. Suggest a concept for new design of tree pruning robot.

CHAPTER 15

SOIL DYNAMICS IN TILLAGE AND TRACTION

1. If tractor forward velocity increases, then soil compaction will?
   Decreases

2. Subsoiling results in increase of soil properties such as
   Soil macro porosity, Air Permeability and Unsaturated Hydraulic Conductivity.

3. Subsoiling results in decrease of soil properties such as
   Soil Bulk density, Penetration resistance

4. The quality of puddling is given by?
   Puddling index

5. Will the indigenous plough inverts the soil? If yes, state the percentage of soil inverted.
   No

6. Mulch tillage can give good yield in the climate of?
   Semi arid to arid climates

7. Mention the types of Minimum tillage practice.
   1. *Strip Processing*
   2. *Wheel tract planting*
   3. *Plough plant*

8. Soil inversion can be indicated by the fraction of?

   $S_i = (W_b - W_a)/W_b$

   S_i – *Indicator for Soil Inversion*

   W_b – *No. of weeds or stubble exposed on the surface after ploughing*

   W_a – *No. of weeds or stubble exposed on the surface before ploughing*

9. Soil shear strength is found by two widely used methods. What are they?

   Direct shear test

   Triaxial test

10. What are the different types of friction involved in soil dynamics?
    Soil metal-friction, Soil-soil friction, and Soil internal friction

11. A. Soil degradation may be caused by physical, chemical and biological factors.

    B. Soil degradation may be caused by physical factors.

    C. Soil degradation may be caused by biological factors.

    (Statement A is alone correct/ All are correct/ Statement C incorrect/ All the Statements are wrong)

    All are correct

12. The corollary of "plants not grow in soft soil" must surely be "and wheels work poor on roads." Whether the statement is incorrect? (Yes/No)

    Yes

13. Soil compaction may be defined as "the compaction of soil mass in a X volume".

    The term X will be (Smaller/ Infinite/ Higher/ Zero)

    Smaller

14. Compacted layers immediately below plowing depth is called?

    Plow-pans

15. Soil compaction is a major factor in degradation of?

    Land

16. Compaction caused by livestock is generally confined to a surface of?

    (50 – 100cm/ 0.5 to 1 cm/ -0.5 to - 1 cm/ 5 - 10 cm)

    5 - 10 cm

17. A. Healthy soils - high levels of organic matter,

    B. Soil with high level of organic matter - more resistant to compaction.

    (A is correct, B is partially correct/ A and B are correct but not related/ B and A are related and correct/ No relation or truth exists in both the statements)

    B and A are related and correct

18. Depth of compaction caused by vehicles is proportional to?

    Axle weight

19. Soil stress is usually smallest close to the surface, and increases with depth. (True/False)

    False

20. Susceptibility to compaction is greater when soil is?

    Moist

21. C_n is a dimensionless ratio in relation with rolling resistance. C_n – 50 for hard soils and 20 for tilled soils, then soft sandy soils may have?

    (35/30/25/15)

    15

22. A. Rain or snowfall can stop only harvesting but not tillage

    B. Rain or snowfall can stop only tillage but not harvesting

    C. Rain or snowfall can stop neither tillage nor harvesting

    D. Rain or snowfall can stop both tillage and harvesting

    (A/B/C/D)

    D

23. Range between field capacity and wilting point is called as? (Actual field capacity/Available water/Runoff/Saturation)

    Available water

24. A factor X is considered important by Scholar A. Scholar B says tillage operation can commence, when X drops to about 80% (70% for clay) of maximum available. Scholar C says that plant encounters severe stress when X drops to 20%. What is X? (Moisture/Heat/Erosion/Efficiency/Irrigation)

    Moisture

25. Tillage is done to manage crop residues and not to control erosion, pests. (True/False)

    False

26. Define Wettability

    Wettability is a measure of the degree to which water will adhere to the surface of a material.

27. Soil moisture is important factor relates the two farm actions including irrigation and (Tillage/Pelletization/Rainfall/Both A and C)

    Tillage

28. Parameters of both the tool and the soil are important in abrasion (True/False)

    True

29. Choose the combination which has only static properties

    A. Macropore space & Momentum

    B. Structure & Texture

    C. Cohesion & Macropore space

    D. All the above

    All the above

30. Scholar A says 'Tensile failure may be exactly the measure of adhesion'. Scholar B denies the statement of scholar A. Scholar C says 'tensile failure may be exactly the measure of cohesion'. Scholar D denies both Scholar A and C statements. Whether Scholar D is correct in his action? (Correct/Incorrect)

    Incorrect

31. A static property comes into play in the response of soil to applied forces (True/False) *False*

32. A. Direct shear methods can be adapted for in situ measurements.

    B. Tensile strength of soil is conceived to be the force that is required to pull the soil apart

    (Both A and B are correct/A is correct nut B is wrong/Both are incorrect/Out of syllabus)

    Both A and B are correct

33. How many numbers of criteria for failure have been established in case of plastic flow?
    (9/6/36/None)

    None

34. A. Coefficient of sliding friction as a dynamic parameter

    B. Adhesion has only single important form of behaviour which is in connection with stickiness.

    C. Adhesion is a dynamic property

    (All three statements are correct/A and B only correct/A and C only correct/C only correct)

    A and C only correct

35. Select the combinations of composite parameters
    A. Penetration and bearing strength

    B. Induced strength and bearing strength

    C. Penetration and bearing strength

    D. A, B and C options

    A, B and C options

36. Apparent specific gravity is given by dividing dry bulk density with?
    (Relative humidity/Density of water/Porosity/Not applicable)

    Density of water

37. Pulverization results from (Tensile failure/Shear failure/Impact forces/All the above)
    All the above

38. Penetration is an action that may be described by a composite behaviour (True/False)
    True

39. A. Dynamic action of soil sliding over a metal surface is the action Y

    B. interaction of soil and metal is highly complex during an action X.

If X and Y represent the same action, then what is the action? (Cohesion/Adhesion/Erosion/Abrasion)

40. Non-continuous tracers, glass-sided box technique, fluorescent tracer materials are associated with (Soil moisture/Soil movement/Soil compaction/Soil porosity)
Soil movement

41. If a tool is coated with a thin coat of material, scratches made by soil particle can be easily detected. What is the coating material? (Varnish/Wood/Petrol/Flex quick)
Varnish

42. Soils with high levels of organic matter are rather more resistant to compaction. (True/False) *True*

43. Rock, roots, or layering in non homogeneous soil may not cause point loading. (True/False) *False*

44. What are three abstract design factors defining the soil manipulation?
Initial soil conditions, shape of the tillage tool and the manner of moving the tool

45. A. Edge shape - refer to the shape of edges
    B. Macro shape - designate shape of the gross surface

    C. Designer don't have a complete control over the shape

    (i. All are correct statements/ii. A and B are correct/iii. C is incorrect/iv. Both ii and iii)

    Both ii and iii

46. Manipulation-shape relation has received emphasis in subsoiler studies. Whether the relation mentioned in the statement is correct? If not what is the correct relation?
Incorrect, Force-shape

47. Manipulation-shape relation has received emphasis in mouldboard plough studies. Whether the relation mentioned in the statement is correct? If not what is the correct relation?

    Correct

48. Mention one of the most direct methods of reducing the frictional resistance of a tool

    (Improve the micro shape/Improve the edge shape/Improve the fuel quality/None of the above)

    Improve the micro shape

49. Micro shape is related with surface roughness (Correct/ Incorrect)

    Correct

50. What is the main reason for puddling operation in paddy cultivation?

51. List out the various puddling aids used in India.

52. Difference between slip and skid

53. What do you know about creep in vehicle movement?

54. Difference between radial ply and bias ply tyres.

55. Select the term associated with Scouring. (Shedding/Self-cleaning/Sliding/All of the above)

    All of the above

CHAPTER 16

GENERAL KNOWLEDGE

1. CIAE stands for

   Central Institute of Agricultural Engineering

2. Indian Society of Agri engineers begin during the year?

   1960

3. Who is the present ICAR-DDG of Agricultural Engineering? (2024)

   Dr. Shyam Narayan Jha

4. Who is the present president of ISAE? (2024)

   Dr. Shyam Narayan Jha, DDG (Agricultural Engineering)

5. Which is the first Agricultural University of India?

   Govind Ballabh Pant Agricultural University, Pantnagar, Uttarkhand

6. Name some NGOs working on Agriculture in India

7. Pokkali rice cultivation is found in the region?

   Central Kerala

8. Potato cultivation is fully mechanized and mostly found in the regions of?

   Punjab and Uttar Pradesh

9. Where does IRRI located?

   International: IRRI - Philippines

   Indian: ISARC - Varanasi

Indian Institute of Rice Research - Hyderabad

National Rice Research Centre - Cuttack, Odissa.

10. What is SMAM?

    The Sub Mission on Agricultural Mechanization

11. Total how many number of KVK's in India? (2020)

    716 KVK's

12. KAU headquartered at?

    Vellanikara, Thrissur

13. Indian Grassland and Fodder Research Institute was situated at?

    Jhansi

14. Where is the Extension Education Institute (Southern region) located?

    Hyderabad

15. Rice bowl of Karnataka

    Thungabhadra

16. Agricultural Minister of India? (2024)

    Shri Shivraj Singh Chouhan

17. What made the groundnut to spread from southern and western states of India to Groundnut - nontraditional states such as Orissa, Bihar, Assam and Uttar Pradesh?

    Technical Mission on Oil

18. What are the macronutrients needed for plants and what role does they have on plant life?

    Primary macronutrients

    N - Nitrogen – Energy metabolism and Protein synthesis

P - Phosphorus - Root growth, flowering stimulation, transportation and storage of energy

K - Potassium - Regulation of water, transportation, photosynthetic capacity

Secondary macronutrients

C - Calcium - Cell wall, cell growth and formation

Mg – Magnesium – Photosynthesis, transportation of phosphorus, storage of sugars

S – Sulfur – Chlorophyll formation, nitrogen metabolism, tissue formation, photosynthesis and protein synthesis

19. Match the following

S.No.	A	M.No.	B
1	Arboriculture	a)	Bees
2	Aviculture	b)	Trees
3	Mariculture	c)	Marine life & Sea food
4	Permaculture	d)	Birds
5	Apiculture	e)	Sustainable Agriculture Developments

Ans. 1-b, 2-d, 3-c, 4-e, 5-a

20. Name a State excelled in Farm Mechanization

Punjab

S.No	Term	Multiplication factor	Symbol
1	Yocto	10^{-24}	y
2	Zepto	10^{-21}	z
3	Atto	10^{-18}	a
4	Femto	10^{-15}	f
5	Pico	10^{-12}	p
6	Nano	10^{-9}	n
7	Micro	10^{-6}	μ
8	Milli	10^{-3}	m
9	Kilo	10^{3}	k
10	Mega	10^{6}	M
11	Giga	10^{9}	G
12	Tera	10^{12}	T
13	Peta	10^{15}	P
14	Exa	10^{18}	E
15	Zetta	10^{21}	Z
16	Yotta	10^{24}	Y

21. Norman E Borlaug is father of

Green Revolution

22. Father of Green Revolution in India

M S Swaminathan

23. Father of White revolution in India (Dr. Verghese Kurien/Mr. Vishal Tewari/ Er. Ayyappan nair/ Agri. Roshan Singh)

Dr Verghese Kurien

24. Dr Verghese Kurien is called by the name of?

Milk Man of India

25. Father of Red revolution

Vishal Tewari

26. Father of Blue Revolution
Dr. Arun Krishnan and Dr. Hirlal Chaudhuri

27. Crystal oscillators are used in watches. (True/False)
True

28. Virulent - not extremely severe or non-harmful in its effects. The statement is wrong - (True/False)
True

29. Lithium-ion batteries can be much (smaller/larger) and lighter than the nickel–cadmium batteries
Smaller

30. Bonfilioli.com is related to what system
Transmission

31. What is WDRA?
Warehousing Development and Regulatory Authority

32. A brand has a set of (tangible/intangible) attributes.
Both tangible and intangible.

33. What is DEMAT?
Dematerialization

34. Manchester of South India is?
Coimbatore

35. The God's own country?
Kerala

36. Garden city of India?
Bangalore

37. City of pearls?
Hyderabad

38. Rice bowl of India?

    Andhrapradesh

39. In earth's continental area, the wetlands covers about the percentage of?

    6.4

40. Jute is mostly grown in which part of the Indian country?

    Eastern Part of India

41. Length of coastal line of India?

    7516.6 km

42. What is the nickname of 'CFC'?

    Wonder chemical

43. Naturally Ventilated Green Houses should not exceed the size of?

    40 m x 40 m

44. Butane at atmospheric pressure and 0^0 C will

    Boils

45. Green Revolution: Rice and Food Grains Production, then White Revolution is?

    White Revolution: Milk Production

46. The warm trade between the body and the climate happens in 4 distinct manners?

    - *Conduction*
    - *Convection*
    - *Radiation*
    - *Vanishing (Sweat and breath)*

47. Expansion of NAAS

    National Agricultural Science Academy Score

48. What is ISSN?

    International Standard Serial Number

49. What is ISBN?

    International Standards Book Number

50. What is meant by CARE? Whether ICAR is a member of CARE?

    Consortium for Academics and Research Ethics. Yes.

51. Match the following

S.No.	A	M.No.	B
1	Pisciculture	a)	Grapevines
2	Viticulture	b)	Fish farming
3	Moriculture	c)	Mulberry farming
4	Permaculture	d)	Mushrooms
5	Fungiculture	e)	Sustainable Agriculture Developments

Ans. 1-b, 2-a, 3-c, 4-e, 5-d

52. Match the following

A	B	X	Y
Lion	Virology	Orange	Fodder crop cultivation
Tiger	Floriculture	Yellow	Earthworms
Peacock	Silviculture	Red	Viruses
Elephant	Olericulture	Blue	Flowers and ornamental plants
Tortoise	Vermiculture	Brown	Vegetables farming

Ans. Lion - Red, Tiger - Blue, Peacock - Orange, Elephant - Brown, Tortoise - Yellow

53. Which animal can fly backwards? (Humming bird/ Parrot/ Elephant/Axolots)

    Humming bird

54. India's largest state by area is?

    Rajasthan

55. Smallest state of India is not the (Delhi/ Goa/ Manipur/ Both A & C)

    Both A & C

56. A. Sikkim was the India's first fully organic state in 2016

    B. Sikkim nestled in the western Himalayas

    (A and B are correct/ A is wrong and B is incorrect/ A and B are error/ B is incorrect)

    B is incorrect

57. India's top farming state is UP (True/False)

    True

58. India's longest route running train was (Mani/ Gita/ Vivek/ Johny)

    Vivek

59. In India. Kolkata metro was the first of its kind and launched (after 2000/ by 2000/ before 2000/ Statement is incorrect)

    Before 2000

60. Height of Ranganathar temple tower, Thiruvarangam, Tiruchirapalli

    About 240

61. State having highest tribal population in India

    Madhyapradhesh

62. Manchester of India

   Mumbai

63. Richest state of India, Ajanta caves locality, Queen of the Deccan, Oxford of the East (Madhya Pradesh, Maharashtra, Gujarat, Jharkhand)

   Maharashtra

64. ICAR was established during (2029/ 1929/ 1959/ 1859)

   1929

65. DARE means (Division of Agricultural Rural Extension/ having enough courage to do something/ Department of Agricultural Research and Education/ Both A and D)

   Department of Agricultural Research and Education

66. Match the following

S. No.	A	M. No.	B
1	King of rice	a)	Padma
2	Irrigated	b)	Basmati
3	Long duration Ponmani	c)	CR 1009
4	Kole land rice	d)	NRRI
5	CRRI	e)	Kerala

   Ans: 1-b, 2-a, 3-c, 4-e, 5-d

67. indiastat – (focused on data/ focused on facts/ focused on india/ focused in value)

   Focused on facts

68. Which is the least or no paddy producing state of India?

69. Name the logo symbolizes wheat in growing stage (Wheat council of India/ Farmer cooperative society of Punjab/ IFFCO/ ICAR)

   ICAR

70. The grain in the ICAR logo was a (Rice/ Wheat/ Maize/ Cumbu)
    Wheat

71. A. NFDB is located at Hyderabad

    B. NFDB is National Fisheries Development Board

    C. TNJFU is headquartered at Nagapattinam

    (A, B and C are correct/ A and B are wrong/ C is wrong/ A is correct and B is incorrect)

    A, B and C are correct

72. Patent in India is valid for how many years?
    20 years

73. Copyright in India is valid for (60 years/ 60 years + authors lifetime/ authors' lifetime + 60 years/ authors lifetime + 20 years)
    authors' lifetime + 60 years

74. Large Cardamom is geotagged by (Sikkim/ Tamilnadu/ Kerala/ Rajasthan)
    Sikkim

75. Current population of India

76. What is the difference between Master of engineering, Master of Science in Engineering and Master of technology?

77. Central Silk Board (CSB) of India was located in the state of?
    Karnataka

78. Bihar is a significant Jute producing state (True/False)
    True

79. Brief the targets of e-Vehicles in India

80. What is eSIM and EID?

81. Difference between

    a. Blurb, abstract and synopsis

    b. DNA and RNA

    c. Shrimp and prawn

    d. Country and nation

    e. Preface and foreword

82. What is the minimum age limit for license (in India) to operate a below 50 cc vehicle? (50/15/16/18)

    16

83. Siruvani water is known for its (Taste/Quantity/Pollutants/Dye)

    Taste

84. Recent UN Climate Change Conference held at?

85. Match the following

S. No.	A	M. No.	B
1	Pokkahboeng	a)	Cotton
2	Blast	b)	Sugarcane
3	Leaf curl	c)	Banana
4	Wilt	d)	Paddy
5	Sigatoka	e)	Potato
6	Scab	f)	Coconut

Ans: 1-b, 2-d, 3-a, 4-f, 5-c, 6-e

86. NSS Day was celebrated on?

87. Match the following

C	A	D	B
Red	Major General	Pepper	above Brigadier
Yellow	Chief Marshal	Cross	above Colonel
Green	Lieutenant General	Cherry	Air, Navy and Army
Blue	Admiral	Leaf	Army
Pink	Chief of Defence	Sticky trap	Air
White	Brigadier	Lilies	Navy

Matching terms in A and B or C and D can make one pair. If both A and B, corresponding C and D are matching, then its called as a set. How many sets can be formed in this? (1/2/9/6)

Ans: 2

C	D	A	B
Red	Cherry	Major General	above Brigadier
Yellow	Sticky trap	Chief Marshal	Air
Pink	Lilies	Lieutenant General	Army
Blue	Cross	Admiral	Navy
Green	Leaf	Chief of Defence	Air, Navy and Army
White	Pepper	Brigadier	above Colonel

88. Difference between cell phone and mobile phone

CHAPTER 17
FARM MACHINERY ECONOMICS AND MANAGEMENT

1. Which is the ongoing five year plan?
    Five year plans stopped by 2017

2. What is the full form of NITI in NITI Aayog?
    National Institution for Transforming India

3. Planning commission of India was replaced by?
    NITI Aayog

4. What is the expansion of VAT?
    Value Added Tax

5. While performing cost analysis, Insurance and shelter can be taken at the rate of?
    2% of purchase value per year

6. Terms in Cost Analysis
    Break even point, Payback period, Net Present Value, Salvage Value, Depreciation, Principle, Return on Investment (ROI), Internal Rate of Return (IRR)

7. Give the Extensively used methods to compute the depreciation
    Straight line method, Declining balance method, and Sum of the years' digit method

8. Name a Government of India Scheme providing insurance cover and financial support to farmers in case of Crop damaged.
    Fasal Bima Yojana, implemented in 2016

9. What is TAR in Cost analysis?
    Total Accumulated Repair

10. What is meant by inflation in economics?
    Decrease in the purchasing power of money, reflected in a general increase in the prices of goods and services in an economy. The converse of inflation is deflation

11. Define the terms GDP, IRR and NPV

12. 'Time value of money' is the term used in economics (True/False)
    True

13. Reduction in value caused by weathering and obsolescence is called as? (Junk value/Insurance/Miscellaneous charge/Depreciation)
    Depreciation

14. Establishment charges: 25% of the total cost of operation. (True/False)
    True

15. Tractor driver cum mechanic is paid at the rate of how many times the wages of a labour? (Approximately 3 times/Exactly the same/Exactly 5 times/Approximately 2 times)
    Approximately 3 times

16. Name the different types of life noted for a machine
    i   *Ownership life*
    ii   *Physical life*
    iii *Useful life*

17. i. Miscellaneous charges   -   a. 6% of initial cost

    ii. Minor repair and maintenance   -   b. 2% of operating cost

    iii. Insurance   -   c. 1% of initial cost

                                       d. None of the above

    (i-c,ii-b,iii-d/i-a, ii-a, iii–d/ i-a, ii-a, iii–b/i-d,ii-a,iii-c)

    i-a, ii-a, iii–d

18. Junk value is approximately assumed to be 50% of the initial cost of the machine. Whether the statement is correct/ incorrect? Also, justify with correct statement if incorrect.
    Incorrect, Junk value is assumed to be 10% of the initial cost of machine.

19. What is GeM?
    (Government e Marketplace/Government eclectic Maintenance/ Government e Mobility/Government e Management)

    Government e Marketplace

20. Branch of economics which is concerned with the use of mathematical methods (especially statistics) in describing economic systems
    Econometrics

21. Indian government's target of doubling the farmer's income by?
    (2016/ 2022/ 2030/ 2030)
    2022

22. By 2023, number of FPO's in India was more than (700/ 7000/ 70001/ 2350)
    7000

23. What is the India's global position on tractor industry?

24. What is the importance of MSP in agriculture?

25. Difference between

    a. Micro economics and macro economics

    b. Fixed cost and variable cost

    c. Production economics and market economics

26. Pradhan Mantri Kisan Samman Nidhi provides farmers an yearly amount of (28000/ 6000/ 12000/ 500)
    6000

27. What are the economical benefits of variable rate technology in Indian context?

28. How does the farm machinery adoption differ between male and female farmers in India?

29. What financial support mechanisms (e.g., subsidies, loans) are available to female farmers for purchasing farm machinery?

30. What is SMAM?
    Sub-Mission on Agricultural Mechanization

31. Match the following

S.No.	A	M.No.	B
1	SMAM	a)	Training in the operation and maintenance of farm machinery.
2	Deen Dayal Upadhyaya Grameen Kaushalya Yojana	b)	Targeted farmers
3	DBT	c)	Subsidies for various types of machinery

32. What is DBT in context of Farm machinery economics? (Dual Benefit Training/ Direct Bank Transfer/ Dense Benefit Transfer/ Department of Banking under Technology)
Direct Benefit Transfer

33. What is APEDA?
Agricultural and Processed Food Products Export Development Authority

34. Difference between
    a. Field efficiency and capacity
    b. Permutation and combination
    c. Management and maintenance
    d. Timeliness cost and efficiency cost
    e. CPP and LPP
    f. Regression and correlation
    e. Optimum design and trial & error
    g. Deterministic and stochastic system

35. Define and explain timeliness cost for farm machinery.

36. How to do LPP in MS-Excel?

37. Internal Rate of Return (IRR) is a method for evaluating (Efficiency of machine/ Profitability of the investment/ Work efficiency of machine/ None)
Profitability of the investment

38. What do you know about confidence limits and significance?

39. Which of the following best defines "uncertainty cost" in the context of machinery management?
    A. The fixed cost associated with initiating a machine production regardless of its outcome

B. The potential financial impact resulting from unpredictable variables affecting the machine.

C. Difference between the predicted and actual costs of a producing the machine

D.   The expenses incurred in mitigating known risks of a machine operation

(A and B/ A only/ D and C only/ B only)

B only

40. Discuss the different types of probability samplings.

41. How Annuities is related with farm machinery?

42. Which of the following best describes the concept of the time value of money?
    A. Money's value decreases over time due to inflation.

    B. A Euro today is worth more than a Euro in the future due to its potential earning capacity.

    C. The value of money remains constant over time.

    D. Future money has a higher value due to increased investment opportunities.

    Correct Answer: B

43. Which of the following is not typically considered an incremental cost when acquiring new farm power tiller?
    (Purchase price of the power tiller/ Additional fuel costs/ Original purchase price of old power tiller/ Training costs for labors)

    Original purchase price of old machinery

44. Describe about Monte Carlo Simulation.

45. Tillage assists in improving the soil structure (True/False)

    True

46. Srinivas' custom hiring center has three types of machinery viz., 3 tractors, 2 combine harvesters, and 4 sprayers. He needs to allocate these machines to three farmers based on their requirements. Farmer Swathi needs 2 tractors and 1 combine harvester, Farmer Saiprasanth needs 1 tractor and 1 sprayer, and Farmer Rajesh needs 1 combine harvester and 2 sprayers. Each farmer must get exactly the type and number of machines they need. No machine can be split between farmers. The allocation should maximize the usage of machinery, minimizing idle machines. Can Srinivas fulfill the requirements of all three farmers with the available machinery? (Yes/No)

    Yes

47. Geethanjali was running a custom hiring center and has 5 types of machinery viz., 5 tractors, 2 combine harvesters, and 3 balers. Farmer Vasuki requires 10 h of tractor, 16 h of combine harvester and 8 h of baler. Farmer Dinesh needs 8 h of tractor, 4 h of combine and 16 h baler. Farmer Pandian needs only tractor for 22 h. Whether Geethanjali can complete the requirements of all 3 farmers in a single day with 8 h of usual working time per day? (Yes/No)

    Yes

48. Gowtham approached a custom hiring centre operated by Rajesh with 3 tractors and 2 trailers. Due to local mishaps, two drivers where on leave, and there was only one driver available at the centre. The other two drivers will be available on the next day. Gowtham needs to transport a material of 3 trailers. Filling time will be 1 hour followed by a running time of 3 h. Emptying time

I negligible. The job has to be completed on single day, cannot proceed with partial works per day. Whether Gowtham meet his requirement on the same day? (Yes/No)

No

49. A village has 50 acres of farm land with 6 months of crop season per year. Raju and Yallappa were planning a custom hiring centre at that village. Tractor operated equipment A has field capacity 0.5 acre per hour and equipment B with 1 acre per hour field capacity. What else data is now required for deciding the count of machinery purchase for an efficient functioning with maximum yield irrespective of farmers co-operation? (No. of farmers in the village/ Village economy/ Timeliness cost/ Raju's family name)

Timeliness cost

50. A nation has decided that, if any manufacturer procuring more than 30% of the spares for machinery from a specified nation as import, then the subsidy will not be eligible for the manufacturer. What may be the reasons behind this?

51. In what way the subsidies for the farm machinery in India are effective?

52. What are the justifications for establishing Agricultural Engineering Department in each state of India?

53. How 6G and 7G can help in future agricultural economy?

54. If automation and robotics are in a vast adoption, may not it create an unemployment for the traditional/skilled workers? How this can be optimized?

55. What are the major reasons for import of farm machinery in India?

CHAPTER 18

FARM IMPLEMENTS AND MACHINERY (PART II)

1. Differential tempering is applied for?
Making cutting tools

2. The capability of mowers to cut the crops at a height above the ground level is?
30 to 100 mm

3. Breaking of corn ears from stem is called?
Snapping

4. In shear cutting type harvest, the plant stem below the cutting plane is loaded as the?
Simply Supported beam

5. For a sharp knife, edge radius will be?
Small

6. Flail mowers and rotary mowers use what type of cutting?
Impact type of cutting

7. When the flail mower moves forward, the tip of the knives follows a non cycloidal path. If the statement is correct, a value of 1 has to be allotted at box A. If the statement is correct a value of 0 has to be allotted on the box A. If another box, B contains a value 10, and values of the both the boxes were added, compared with box B, the value will be?
Same as of box B

8. What are the terms involved in mechanics of knife cutting a typical plant stem?

   Plastic deformation, Stem buckling, Compression, Shear strength, Tensile stress, Tension, Failure

9. Peak force on harvest cutting reduces by oblique cutting, as the plant material is sheared progressively. (True/False)

   True

10. Person A says to Person B that "in a sugarcane crusher, the rollers rotate in the direction of clockwise". Person B says to Person X that Person A is wrong in his statement. But the person X went to Person A and said that Person A's statement is correct. Person Y was now in the position to tell whose action is right. What Person Y should tell?

    Person B is right in his saying and action, therefore Person A's statement is wrong

11. In planters, for power transmission from wheels, the gears used are made from a material of advancement and better performance. Name the material.

    Plastic gears

12. Vegetable Harvesters are available in foreign countries for many of the crop. Name the most crops.

    Capsicum, Chilly, Cucumber, Cabbage, Carrot, Garlic, Turmeric, Tomato, Potato, Onion, Tapioca (Cassava), Spinach/Greenleaf,

13. The wind speed and air temperature should be in what range in case of aerial spraying?

    Wind Speed - 3 to 16 km/h and Temperature below 32⁰C

14. Which is the most common mean diameter for sprayer or nozzle's particle size reference?

    VMD

    (VMD>SMD>AMD>GMD)

15. What may be the construction materials in the interiors of electric motor?

    Copper, Silicon steel

16. Most of the Coconut related machineries were invented in a South Indian Institute. Name the institute which belongs to ICAR.

    CPCRI, Kasaragod

17. Polyethylene can withstand a temperature of 85^0C only, whereas Teflon can withstand temperature up to

    210^0 C

18. Mention the important property of hydraulic fluid.

    Viscosity

19. Desertification is a?

    Minor Surface corrosion

20. In roller type fertilizer distributor, what is the material used for roller making to avoid corrosion problems?

    Neoprene

21. In V belts, if diameter increases the sheave groove angle will?

    Increases

22. Types of Roller chains are?

    Standard pitch

    Double pitch

23. The materials of construction of Tractor Pulley are?

    Cast iron, Cast Steel or Compressed paper

24. The most commonly used seeder for horticulture is Random seeder. (True/False)?

    True

25. The Multicrop planter is developed by CIAE. (True/False)?

    True

26. Onion can be harvested by two mechanical methods. Name them.

    Digging and Top lifting

27. Field Capacity of Naveen Dibler is?

    0.02 to 0.03 ha/h

28. How many types of fertilizer broadcasters are available for horticulture?

    5 types

29. One of the power tiller operated machinery, which is used for lopping tall branches in tree is called as?

    Tree lopping machine

30. What is the useful life of electric motor?

    15 years

31. Calibration of sprayers refers to Chemical application rate adjustment in terms of L/Ha. The statement is made by professor. But the student refused it. But another professor said that student was not correct. Now who all are correct in their statements?

    Both the professors

32. What are types of green manure tramplers?

    Disc type

    Slat type

33. Which is law is associated with chaff cutter design?

    Duffees law

34. Oxen pushed Gallic Mowing Cart was developed on the period of

    200 BC

35. What is SMV?

    Slow Moving Vehicles

36. Multirow Drill for germinated seeds is related to the International Institute?

    IRRI, Philippines

37. What are the different types of balers?

    1. Round balers

    2. Square balers

38. Sugarcane Planters are powered by?

    Animal and Tractor

39. (A) Anvil is associated with a deflector nozzle.

    (B) Anvil is the iron block of metal. (Both A and B are false/ A is true and B is false/ Both A and B are true/ None of the above)

    Both A and B are true

40. What is Duplex pump?

    Its is a reciprocating pump with two pumping cylinders acting parallel.

41. Decoration of an object with depressed or raised design is called as what?

    Embossing

42. What are the criteria for sprayer selection?

Table No. 2 Selection of Sprayers

S. No	Sprayer type	Preferred Application Area
1	Dusters	Arid and Semi arid region (wherever the water source is scarce)
2	High Volume Spraying	400 liters of spray liquid per hectare
3	Low Volume Spraying	5 - 400 liters of spray liquid per hectare
4	Ultra low volume Spraying	Less than 5 liters of spray liquid per hectare
5	Foot & Rocking Sprayer	Bushy crops and Small trees
6	Knapsack Sprayer	Field Crops, Hilly regions, Waterlogged fields
7	Powered Knapsack Sprayers	Field Crops, Bushy Crops and Small trees, Hilly regions, Waterlogged fields
8	Multipurpose farm Sprayers	Diversified farming

43. Radius gauge can check which of the following surfaces? (Concave/ Convex/ Both/ Flat)

    Both

44. What are strakes?

    Assembly of metal lugs

45. Stone trap is associated with harvesting and collection units. (True/False)

    True

46. Give the different types of nozzles with usage.

Table no.3 Nozzle types and Usage

S. No	Nozzle	Usage
1	Solid cone	Spot spraying, Herbicidal spraying in lawns
2	Flat fan	Herbicidal applications
3	Flooding	Herbicides, Fertilizer spraying
4	Hollow cone	Insecticidal and Fungicidal applications
5	Triple action	High volume, Low volume, Tractor operated spraying (Both the uses of solid cone, hollow cone, jet type)

47. Leaf stage seedlings are transplanted by transplanter when leaf count is?

    (Not less than 6/Not less than 2/No more than 6/Both B and C)

    Both B and C

48. (A) Crank or rotary mechanism is used in the transplanters

    (B) Walking type transplanters uses Crank type

    (C) Riding type transplanters uses Crank type

    (D) Rotary mechanism has eccentric planetary gears and Crank type mechanism uses three bar linkages

    (A is true and other statements are false/A and B are true, other statements are false/All are true except statement D/Statement C is only true)

    All are true except statement D

49. **Match the following**

S. No.	A	M. No	B
1	Wind	a	Weeding
2	UAVs	b	India
3	Inter and Intra row	c	Chennai
4	Tractor export	d	Rotor

Ans.: 1 – c, 2 – d, 3 – a, 4 – b

50. **Match the follwoing**

S. No.	A	M. No	B
1	Calorific value	a	Solar energy
2	Lux	b	Syn gas
3	CTF	c	Weight
4	Disc plough	d	Farming

Ans.: 1 - b, 2 - a, 3 - d, 4 - c

51. **Match the pair suitably**

S. No.	A	M. No	B
1	Cam	a	Evaluation
2	Rack	b	Follower
3	Ergonomics	c	Mahindra
4	Testing	d	Traction
5	Coconut	e	Robotics
6	Mahindra	f	Safety
7	Farm Power	g	Farm Machinery
8	Mechatronics	h	Arecanut
9	Spices	i	Pinion
10	Tillage	j	Plantation crop

Ans.: 1 - b, 2 - i, 3 - f, 4 – a, 5 - h, 6 - c, 7 - g, 8 – e, 9 – j, 10 - d

52. Match the following

S. No.	A	M. No.	B
1	BLDC	a	Biogas
2	BDTC	b	Engine
3	BDC	c	Bharat
4	BLSDC	d	Servo motor
5	BS VI	e	Motor

Ans.: 1 - e, 2 - a, 3 - b, 4 - d, 5 - c

53. Match the following

S. No.	A	M. No.	B
1	Controlled traffic farming	a	Application Losses
2	UAV's	b	Drudgery
3	Driverless tractor	c	Soil compaction
4	Organic farming	d	Unemployment
5	Startups	e	Residual effect

Ans.: 1 - c, 2 - a, 3 - b, 4 - e, 5 - d

54. Match the following

S. No.	A	M. No.	B
1	Soil resistance	a	Actual field capacity
2	Cutting force	b	Field capacity
3	Seed rate	c	Hopper
4	Crop spacing	d	Harvesting blade
5	Angle of repose	e	Tillage
6	Time taken	f	Weeder

Ans.: 1 - e, 2 - d, 3 - b, 4 - f, 5 – c, 6 - a

55. **Match the following**

S. No.	A	M. No.	B
1	Soil bin	a	Soil
2	Patternator	b	Tillage tool
3	Bicycle ergometer	c	Nozzle
4	Dynamometer	d	Movement of air
5	Anemometer	e	Human
6	Cone penetrometer	f	Tractor

Ans.: 1 - b, 2 - c, 3 - e, 4 - f, 5 – d, 6 - a

56. **Match the following**

S. No.	A	M. No.	B
1	Folding rule	a	Concave and Convex
2	Radius gauge	b	Angle
3	Mitre gauge	c	Angle
4	Sine bar	d	Clearance
5	Digital Universal Caliper	e	Distance
6	Feeler gauge	f	Length of work piece

Ans.: 1 - e, 2 - a, 3 - b, 4 - c, 5 – f, 6 - d

57. Name the Horticultural Tools

Axe, Dah, Billhook, Sword

Budding Knife, Grafting Knife, Pruning/Slashing Knife, Chopping knife, Cutting knife

Scissors, Secateurs, Shear

Chain saw, Hedge trimmer

String trimmer

Crow bar

58. Chisel end of Crowbar can be hardened to?

350 – 450 HB

59. In fruit harvesters, the net for holding the cut fruit is made of?
Nylon

60. Improved Plastic Paddy Drum Seeder is developed by?
TNAU

61. 150 to 200 man hours are needed for harvesting one acre of paddy. (True/False)
True

62. Mention the two major categories of sickles.
Serrated type and plain (non serrated type)

63. Naveen and Vaibhav are the names of (Hard disk/Sickles/Farm labours in China/Indian authors)
Sickles

64. What is the use of Dah?
Cutting trees and shrubs

65. Debarker is the machine used for removing the bark from the trees. (True/False)
True

66. (A) Bill hook is associated with lopping of branches

(B) Bill hook is used as plant protection aid

(Both the statements are true/ Both are incorrect statements/ B is correct and A is wrong/ None of the above)

None of the above

67. Match the following

S. No.	A	M. No.	B
1	Trowel	a	Cutting
2	Hatchet	b	Transplanting
3	Grass shear	c	Cutting
4	Hedge shear	d	Lifting
5	Jack	e	Holding
6	Jig	f	Pruning

Ans.: 1 - b, 2 - c, 3 - a, 4 - f, 5 – d, 6 - e

68. Does research divisions of private companies are more efficient than government research institutes? Why?

69. How far does driverless tractor may work in India?

70. Will organic/natural farming reduces the importance of farm machinery?

71. Write an outline for design and development of RF controlled orchard sprayer.

72. List out some immediate needs in farm machinery sector of India.

73. Why combined harvesting operations are better than individual works?

74. List out the machinery available in hill regions of India.

75. Find out a package of machinery for protected cultivation for flowers.

76. What you know about KERA method?

77. Is PORA method is drilling option? (Yes/No)
    Yes

78. Drilling is dropping of seeds in furrow (True/False)

    True

79. Dibbling applied not to vegetable and wheat. (True/False)

    False

80. Row to row spacing ≠ Hill to hill spacing in Hill Dropping (True/False)

    True

ABBREVIATIONS

AE – Assistant Engineer

AEE – Assistant Executive Engineer

AICRP - All India Coordinated Research Project

AMD - Arithmetic Mean Diameter

API - American Petroleum Institute

API - Application Programming Interface

AMIE - Associate Member of Institution of Engineers

ANN - Artificial Neural Network

ASHRAE - American Society of Heating, Refrigeration, and Air Conditioning Engineers

ATP - Adenosine TriPhosphate

BCC – Bio Chemical Conversion

BDTC - Biogas Development and Training Centre

BIS - Bureau of Indian Standards

BEE - Bureau of Energy Efficiency

BMI - Body Mass Index

BoS - Balance of System

CAD - Computer Aided Design

CNN - Convolutional Neural Network

CAAST - Centre for Advanced Agricultural Science and Technology

CDB – Coconut Development Board

CNG - Compressed Natural Gas

CoP - Coefficient of Performance

CSIR - Council of Scientific and Industrial Research

CSR - Corporate Social Responsibility

CTF - Controlled Traffic Farming

CoViD 19 - Corona Virus Disease of 2019

CW – Clock Wise

CCW – Counter Clock Wise

DGPS - Differential Global Positioning System

DDT – Dichloro Diphenyl Trichloroethane

DEM - Digital Elevation Model

DSM - Digital Surface Model

DRIS - Diagnosis and Recommendation Integrated System

EC - Energy Conservation

ECBC - Energy Conservation Building Code

EE – Energy Efficiency

EE –Executive Engineer

EED - Energy Efficient Design

ESA - Ergonomics and Safety in Agriculture

ECG - ElectroCardioGram

EMG – ElectroMyoGram

ESP 32 – Espressif32

FAO - Food & Agricultural Organization

FC – Flight Controller

FCI - Food Corporation of India

FTS - Fischer-Tropsch Synthesis

FIS - Field Information System

FIM - Farm Implements and Machinery

FRP - Fibre Reinforced Plastic

FSSAI - Food Safety and Standards Authority of India

GOOGLE - Global Organization of Oriented Group Language of Earth

GMD - Geometric Mean Diameter

GHG - Green House Gas

GIS - Geographical Information System

GI - Galvanized Iron

GI - Geographical Indication

GPS - Global Positioning System

GLCM - Grey Level Co occurrence Matrix

GUI - Graphical User Interface

HRT - Hydraulic Retention Time

HVAC - Heating Ventilation and Air Conditioning

IC – Internal Combustion

IC – Internal Communication

ICE - Internal Combustion Engine

IDP – Institutional Development Plan

IEA - International Energy Agency

IEI – Institute of Engineers

ILO – International Labour Organization

IMU - Inertial Measurement Unit

IPCC - Intergovernmental Panel on Climate Change

IPR - Intellectual Property Rights

IRC – International Rice Congress

IRRI - International Rice Research Institute

IRRI - Indian Rice Research Institute

ICMR - Indian Council of Medical Research

kVA –kilo Volt Ampere

KNN - K Nearest Neighbors

KYC - Know Your Customer

LASER - Light Amplification by Stimulated Emission of Radiation

LEV – Low Emission Vehicle

LiPO – Lithium Polymer

LWR - Long Wave Radiation

mAh – milli Ampere hour

mAP - mean Average Precision

MGNREGA - Mahatma Gandhi National Rural Employment Guarantee Act

NAAC - National Assessment and Accreditation Council

NAHEP - National Agricultural Higher Education Project

NDDB - National Dairy Development Board

NDVI - Normalized Difference Vegetation Index

OECD - Organization for Economic Cooperation and Development

OSHA - Occupational Safety and Health Act/Administration

PA - Precision Agriculture

PAR - Photosynthetically Active Radiation

PET - Polyethylene Terephthalate

PMU - Power Management Unit

PV – Photovoltaics

PWM – Pulse Width Modulation

RMB - Reversible Mould Board Plough

ROPS - Roll Over Protection System

SAVI – Soil Adjusted Vegetation Index

SMV - Slow Moving Vehicle

SSNM – Site Specific Nutrient Management

SVM - Support Vector Machine

SMD - Sauter Mean Diameter

SAH - Solar Air Heating

SHGC - Solar Heat Gain Coefficient

SWR - Short Wave Radiation

TCC – Thermo Chemical Conversion

TSS - Total Suspended Solids

TGA - Thermo Gravimetric Analyzer

VCR - Vertical Conveyor Reaper

VMD - Volume Mean Diameter

VLoS – Visual Line of Sight

VRT - Variable Rate Technology

VToL – Vertical Take-off and Landing

WGS - World Geodetic System

WS - Wide Span

REFERENCES

1. John A Duffie, William A Beckman, 2013, Solar Engineering for Thermal Processes, Interscience Publication, 9780470873663

2. Anonymous, 2012, ICAR hand book on Agricultural Engineering, Indian Council of Agricultural Research-New Delhi, 978-8171641345

3. Martin Helander, 2005, A Guide to Human Factors and Ergonomics, 978-0415282482

4. M.L.Mehta, S.R.Verma, S.K.Mishra, V.K.Sharma, 2016, Testing and Evaluation of Agricultural Machinery, Daya Publishing, 978-9351309789

5. Guangnan Chen, 2018, Advances in Agricultural Machinery and Technologies, CRC Press, Taylor and Francis Group,

6. Surendra Singh, 2007, Farm machinery Principles and applications, Indian Council of Agricultural Research

7. S C Mandhar, Mechanization of Horticulture, , Daya Publishing House, Astral International Pvt Ltd., 9788170358923

8. Sathyajith Mathew, 2006, Wind Energy: Fundamentals, Resource Analysis and Economics, Springer, 978-3-540-30905-5

9. John B. Liljedahl, Paul K. Turnquist, David W. Smith, Makoto Hoki, 1989,Tractor & Power Units, Van Nostrand Reinhold, New York, 978-1-4684-6634-8

10. K. Srinivasan, Sanjeev Kumar Singh, V.V. Narayanan, L.Geetha Lakshmi, 2015, Tractors and Agricultural Machinery , New India Publishing Agency, 9789385516108

11. Sarbjit Singh, 2018, Important Information in Biogas Technology, Department of Renewable Energy Engineering, Punjab Agricultural University

12. Kanafojski, T. Karwowski, 1976, Agricultural Machines: Theory and Construction Vol. 2, Crop Harvesting Machinery

13. Ajit K. Srivastava, Carroll E. Goering, Roger P. Rohrbach, Dennis R. Buckmaster, 2006, Engineering Principles of Agricultural Machines, American Society of Agricultural and Biological Engineering

14. Prabir Basu, 2013, Biomass Gasification, Pyrolysis and Torrefaction, Elsevier

15. Donnel Hunt, 2013, Farm Power and Machinery Management, Scientific International Pvt Ltd, 978-9381714270.

16. D.R.Hunt 1986. Engineering Models for Agricultural Production. AVI Pub. Co., Westport, CT, USA, 978-0870554940

17. Ashok G Powar, Vijay V Aware, 2020, Farm Machinery and Power: A Glossary, New India Publishing Agency, 978-9390175390.

18. Shesh Nath Rawat, Jagdish S. Nikhade, 2010, Question Bank on Agricultural Engineering, Jain Brothers, 978-8183600187

19. S Vijay Kumar, Pramod Kumar, Muzaffar Hasan, S. Mangaraj, R.K. Shani, N.S. Chandel, S Syed Imran, 2019, Objective

Type Questions on Farm Machinery & Power And General Agriculture, Jain Brothers, 978-8194413707

20. Jagdishwar Sahay, 2020, Elements Of Agricultural Engineering, Standard Publishers and Distributors, 978-8180142048

21. Fareed Shakhatreh, 2011, The Basics Of Robotics, Lahti University of Applied Sciences

22. Tatsuro Muro, Jonathan O'Brien, 2004, Terramechanics: Land Locomotion Mechanics, A.A. Balkema Publishers, 905809572X.

23. R. H. Macmillan, 2002, The Mechanics of Tractor - Implement Performance: Theory and Worked Examples, University of Melbourne

24. W.R Gill, G.E Vanden Berg, 2013, Soil Dynamics in Tillage And Traction, Scientific Publishers (India), 978-8172338039

25. Osamu Kitani, 1999, CIGR Handbook of Agricultural Engineering, Volume V Energy and Biomass Engineering, CIGR–The International Commission of Agricultural Engineering, American Society of Agricultural Engineers, 0-929355-97-0

26. C.R.Mehta, Adarsh Kumar, L P Gite, K N Agrawal, 2022 Textbook of Ergonomics and Safety in Agriculture, Indian Council of Agricultural Research, 978-8171642342.